I0462953

FLOWER
COLORING BOOK

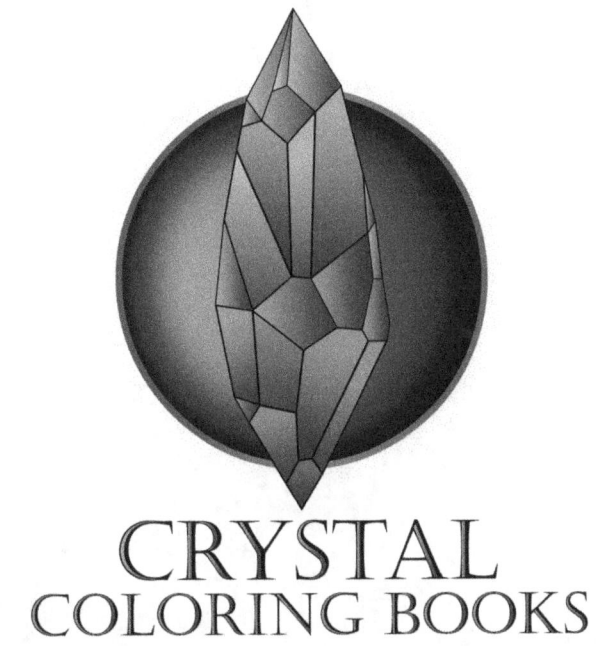

CRYSTAL
COLORING BOOKS

ISBN: 9781081136796

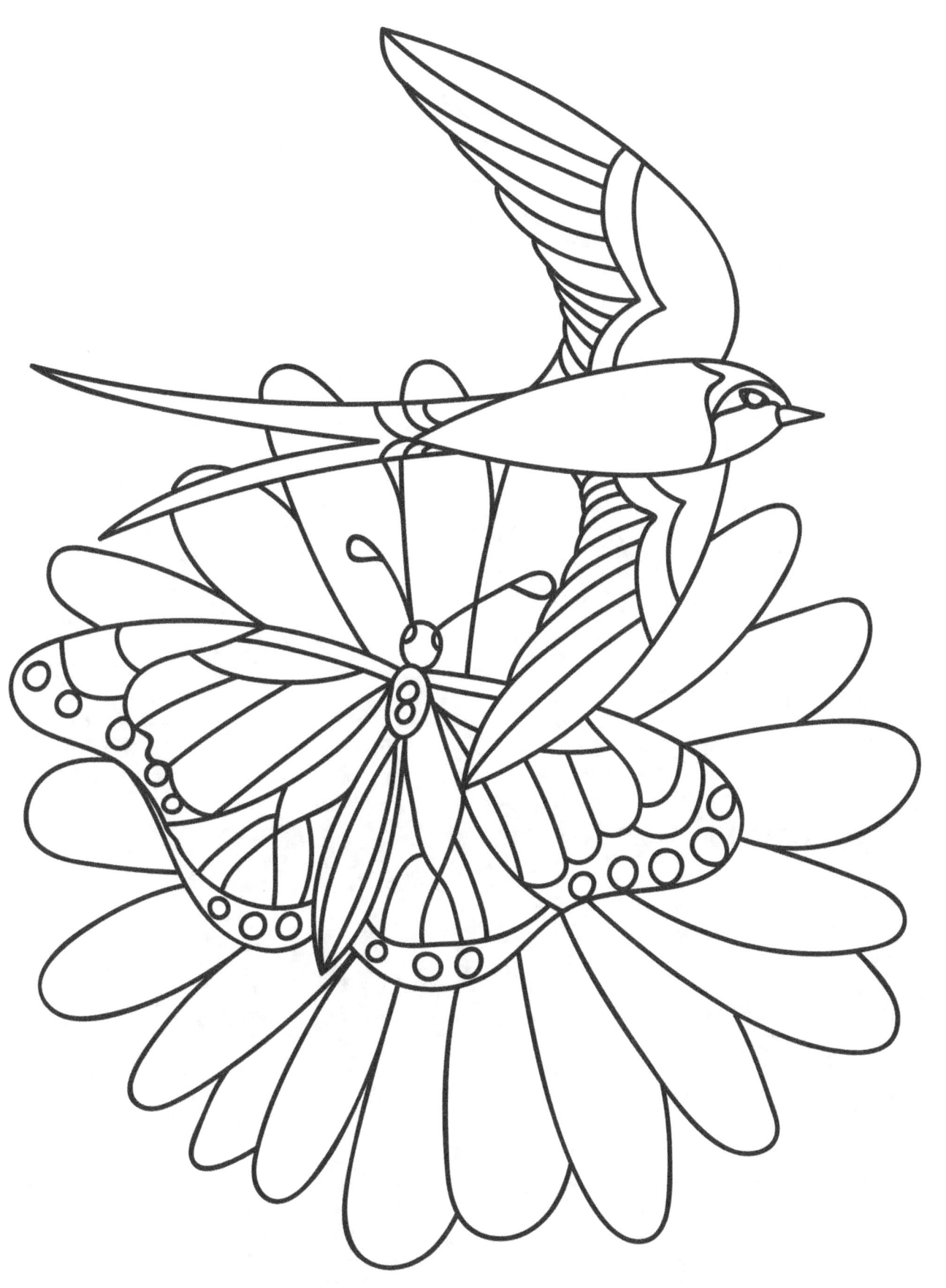

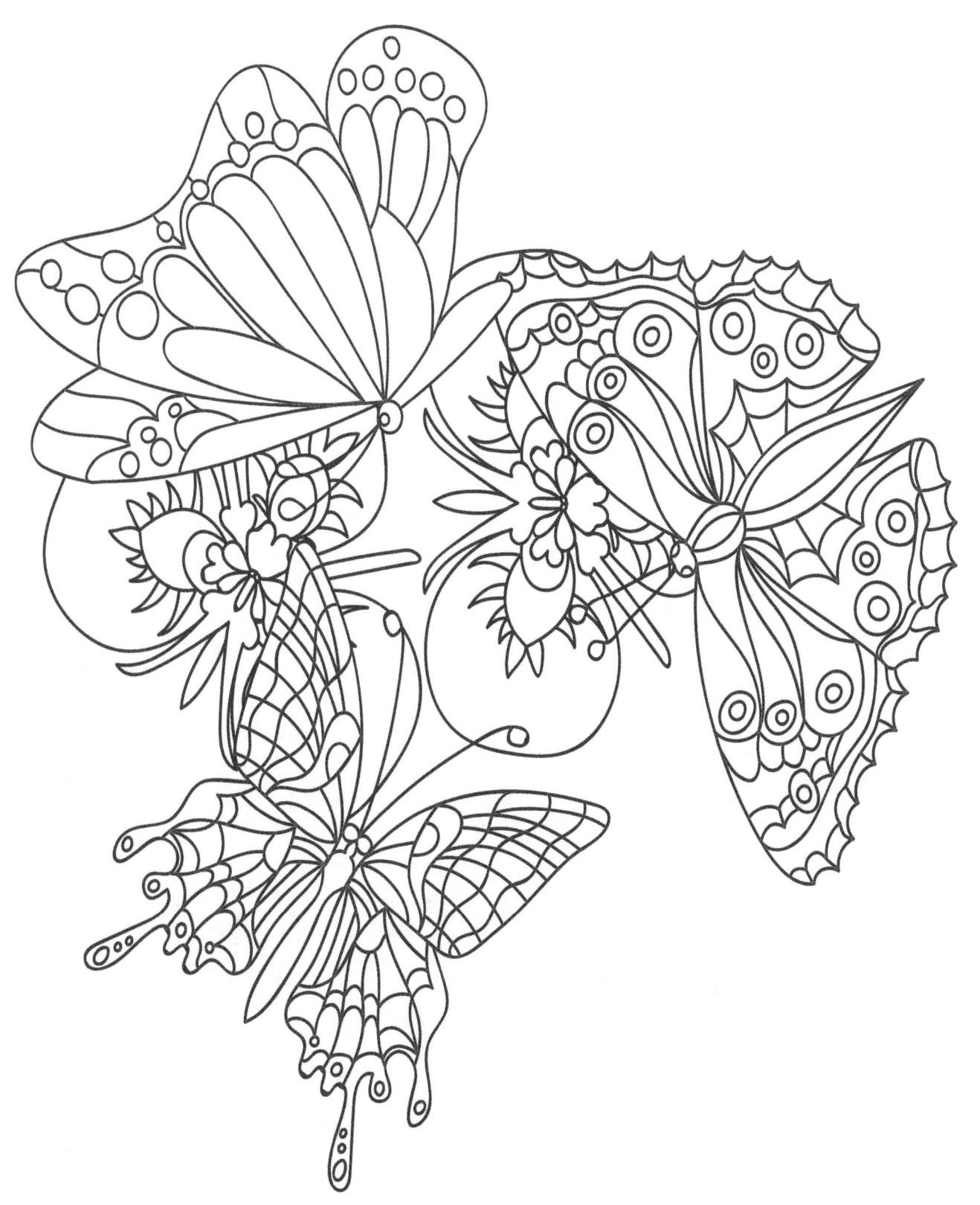

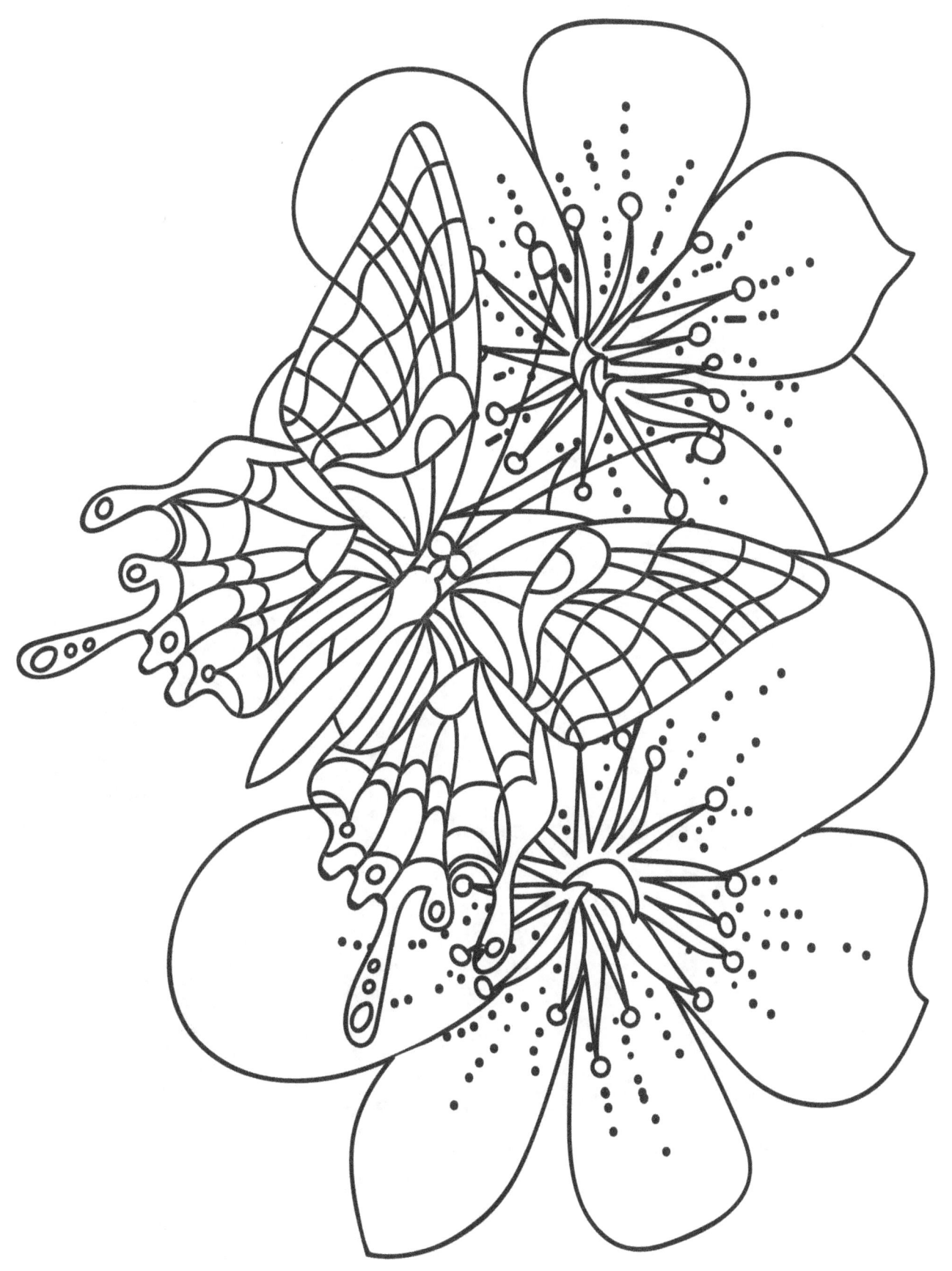

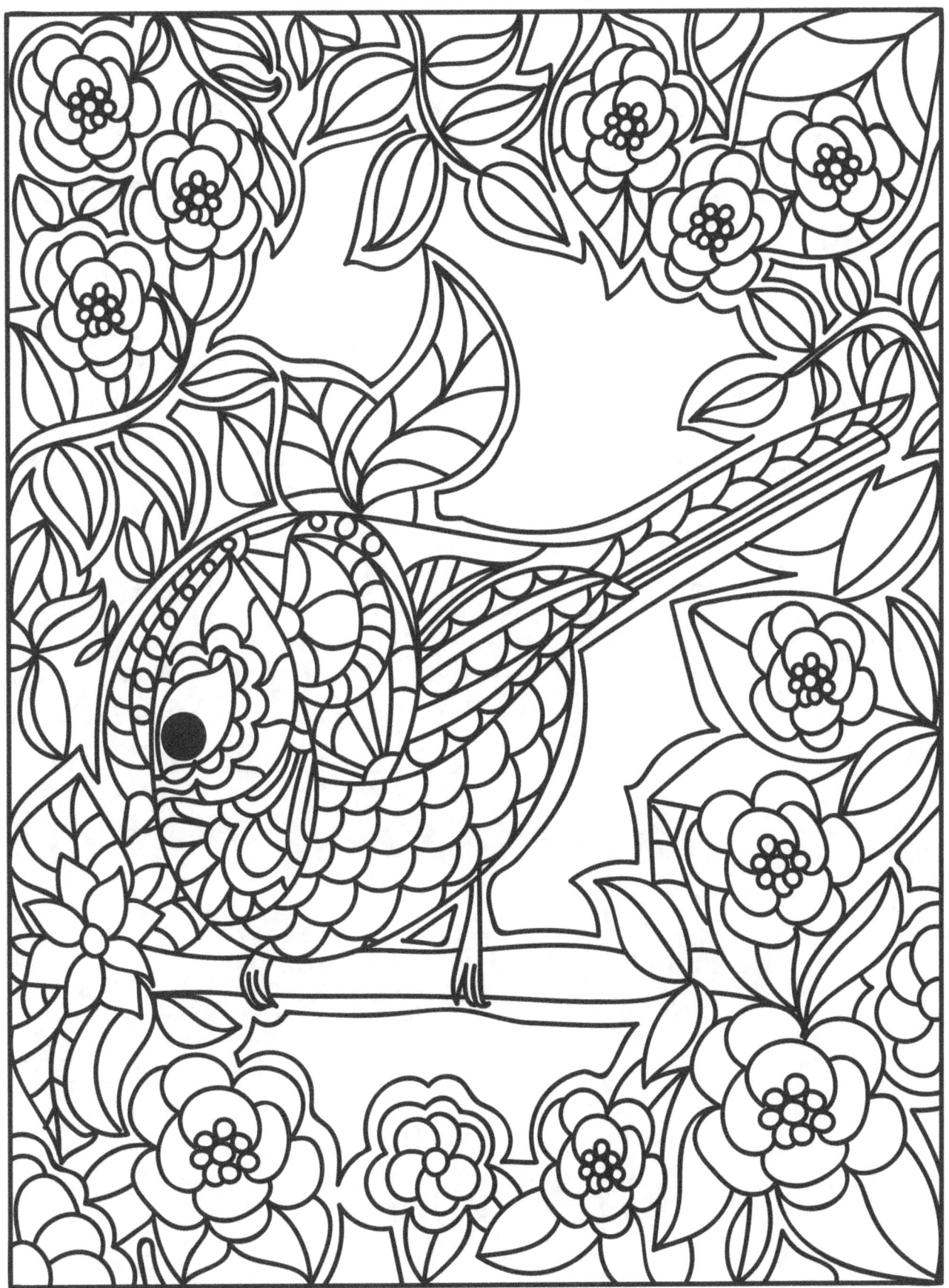

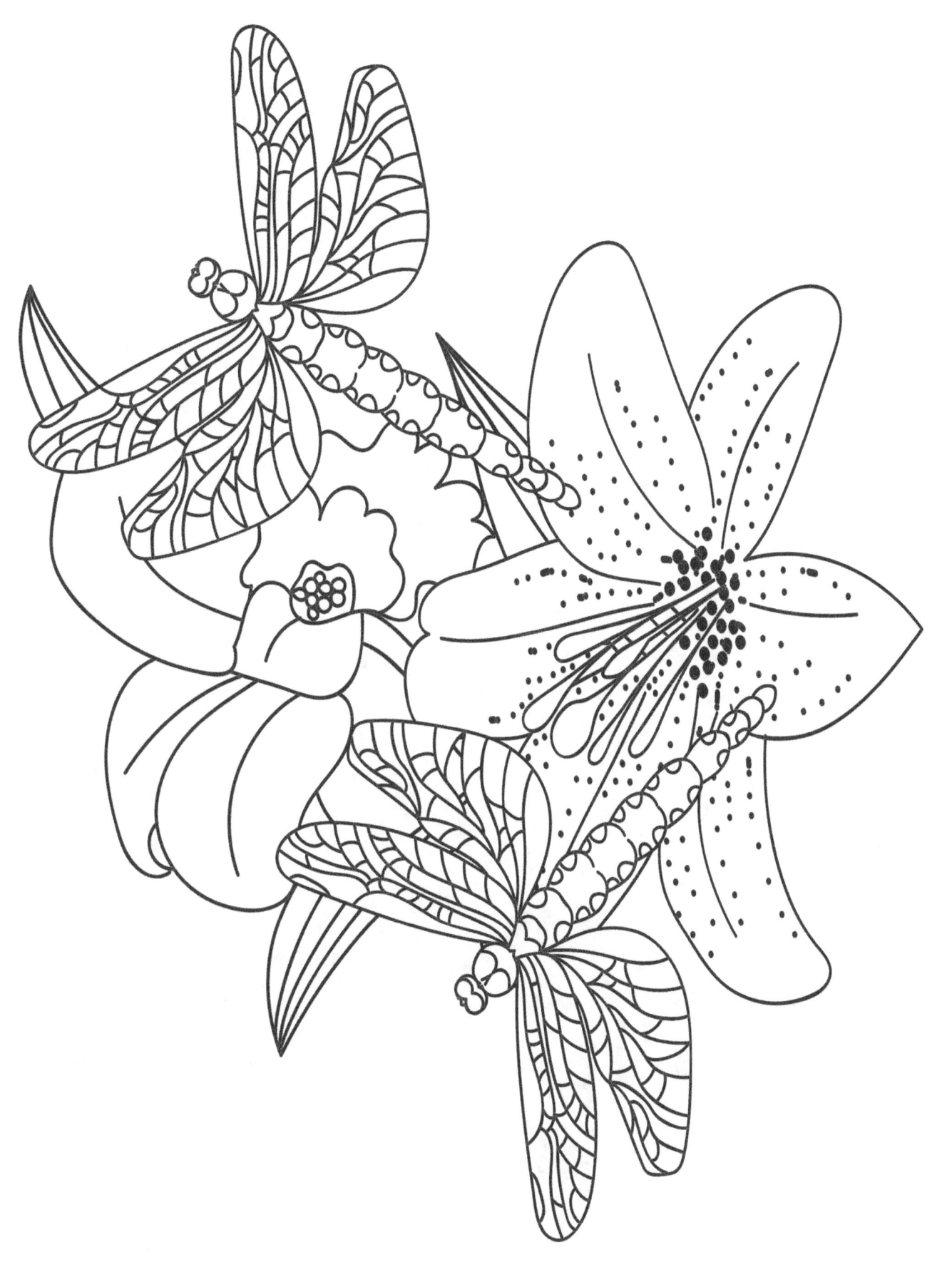

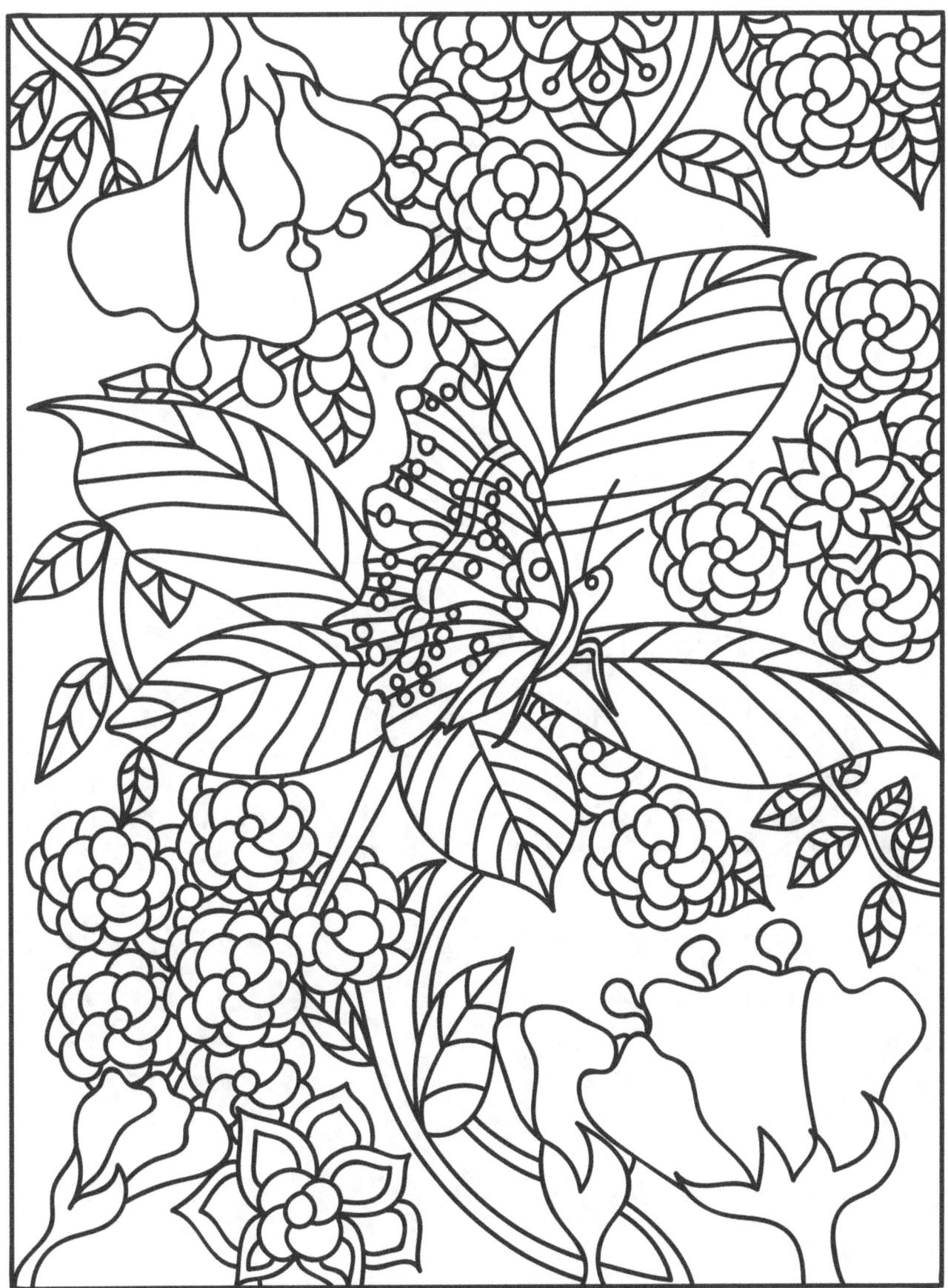

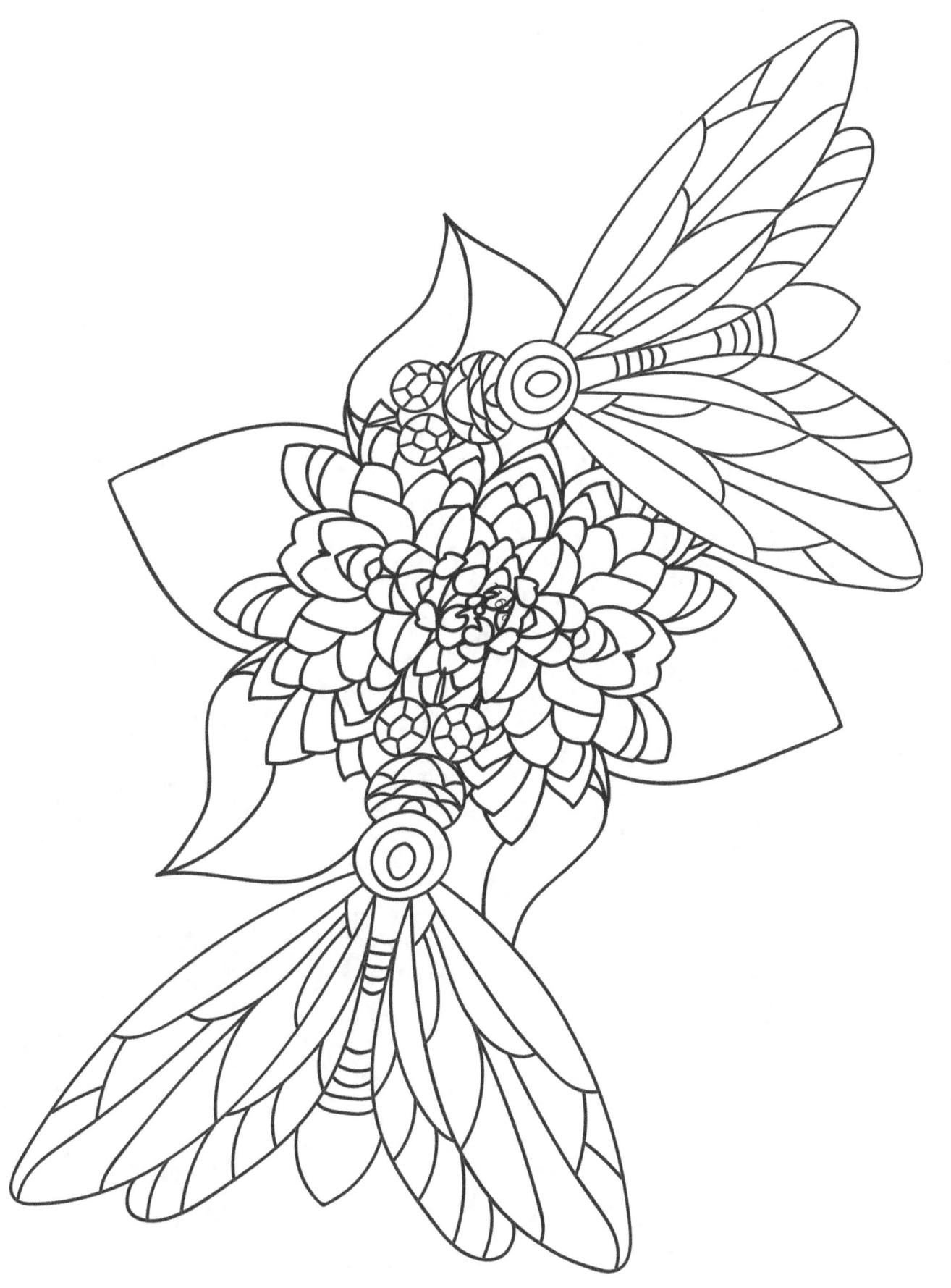

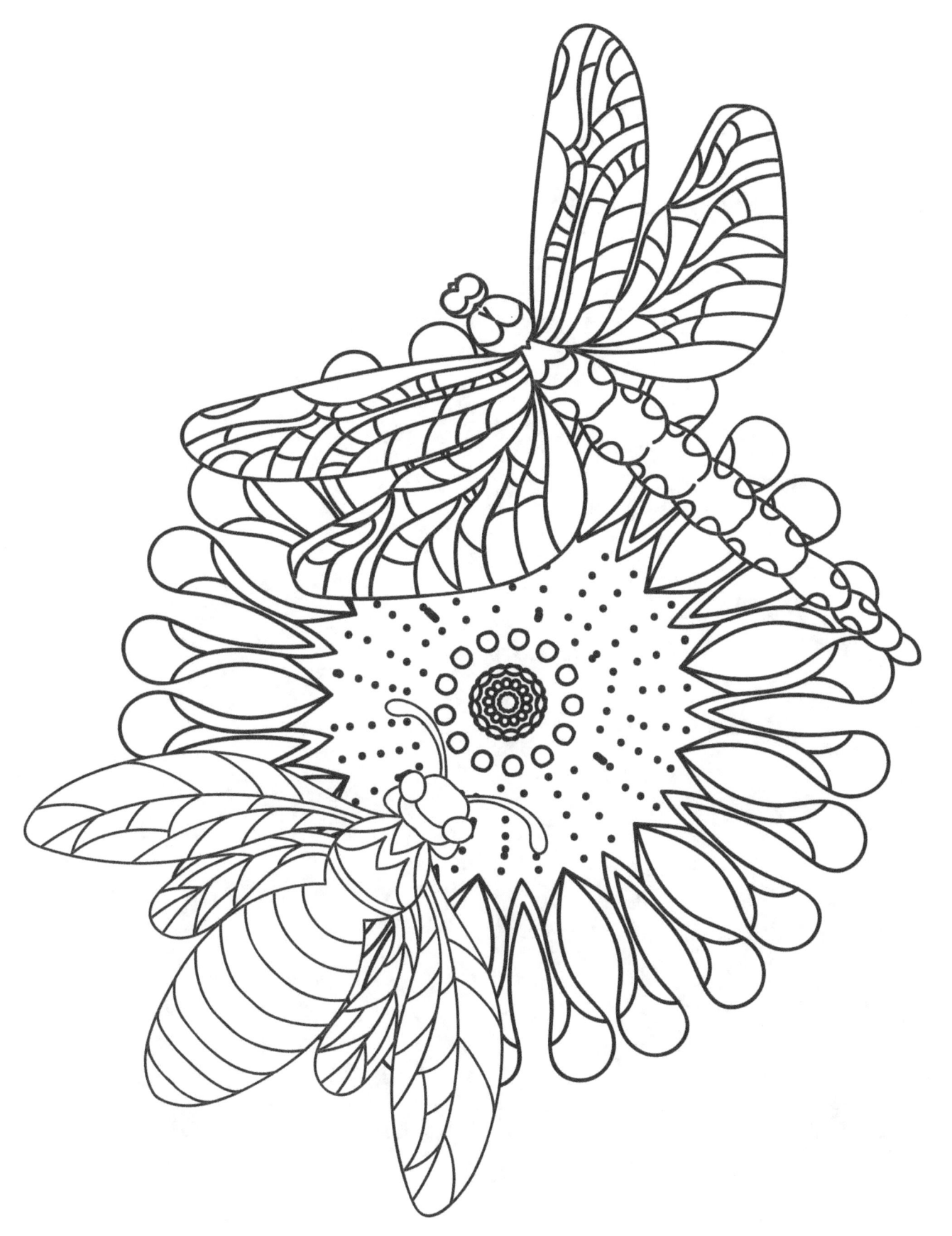

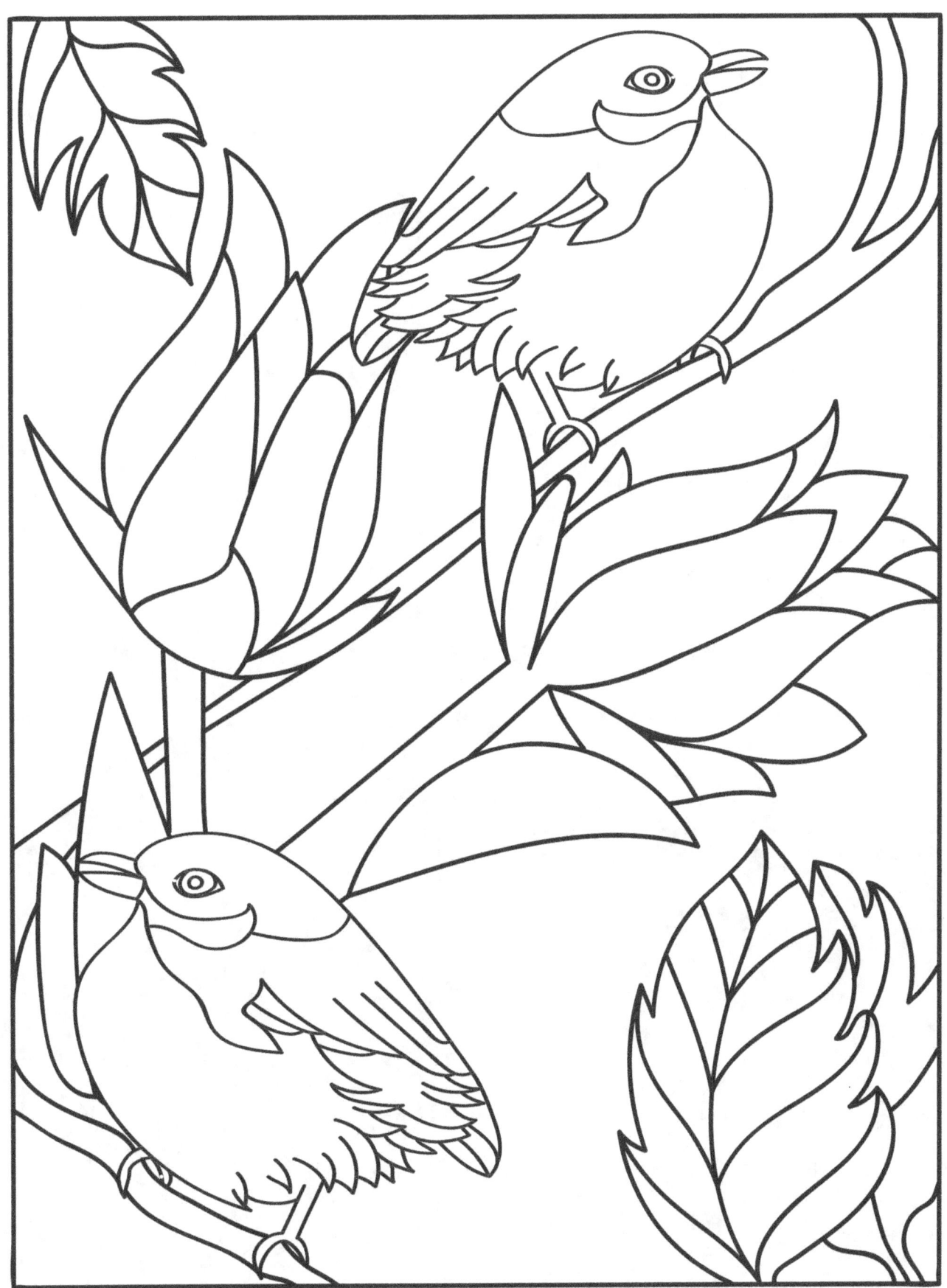

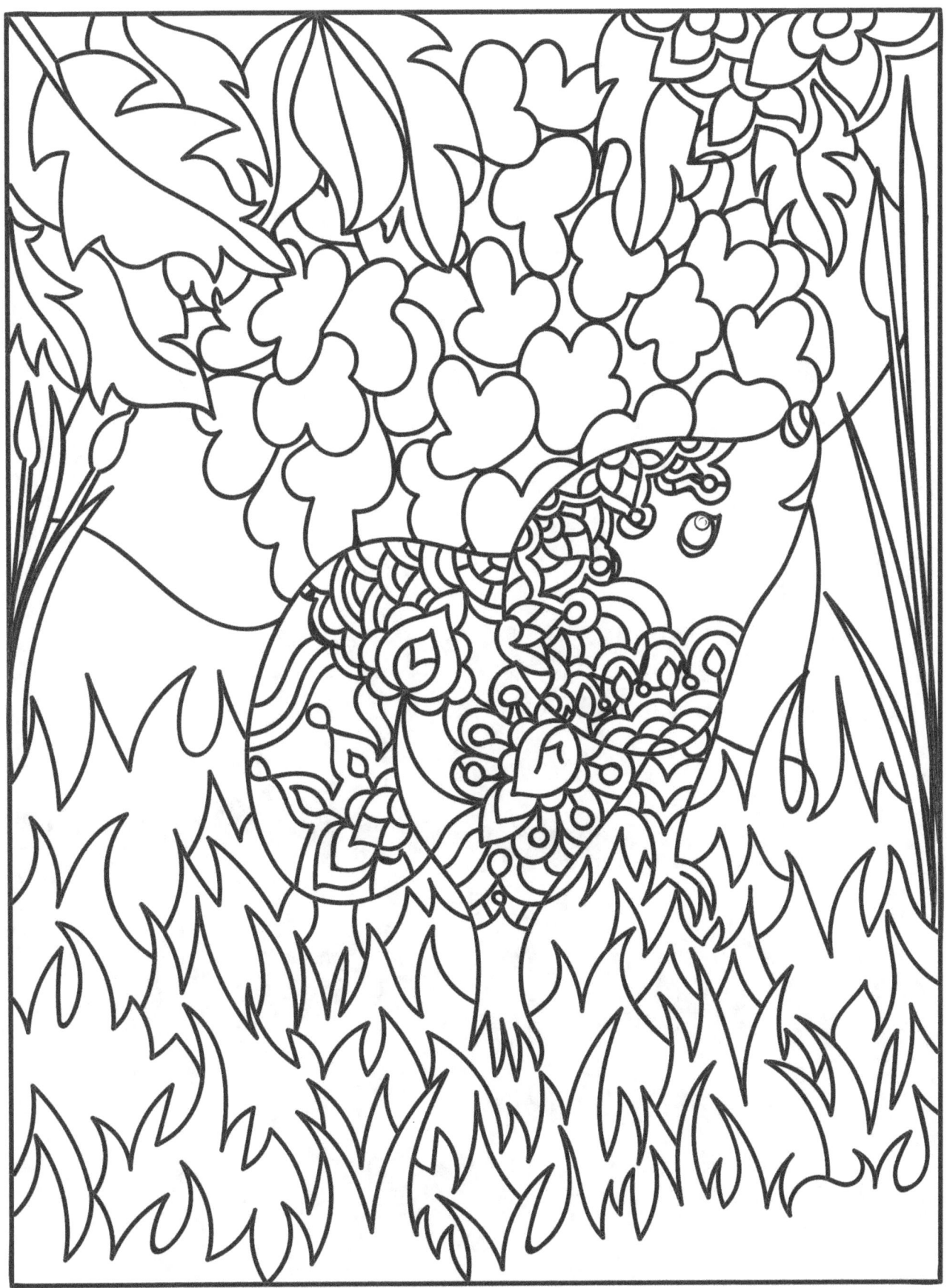

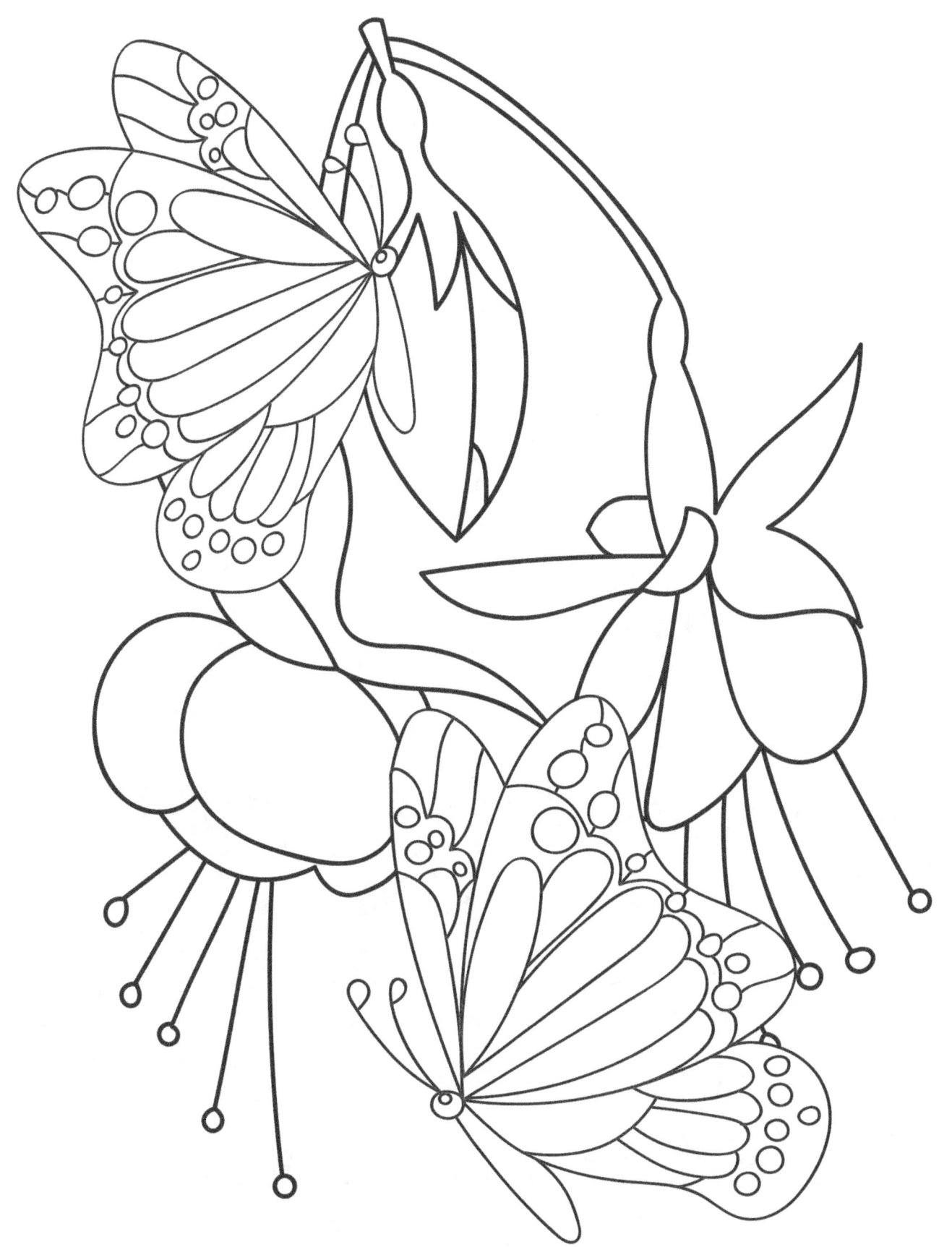

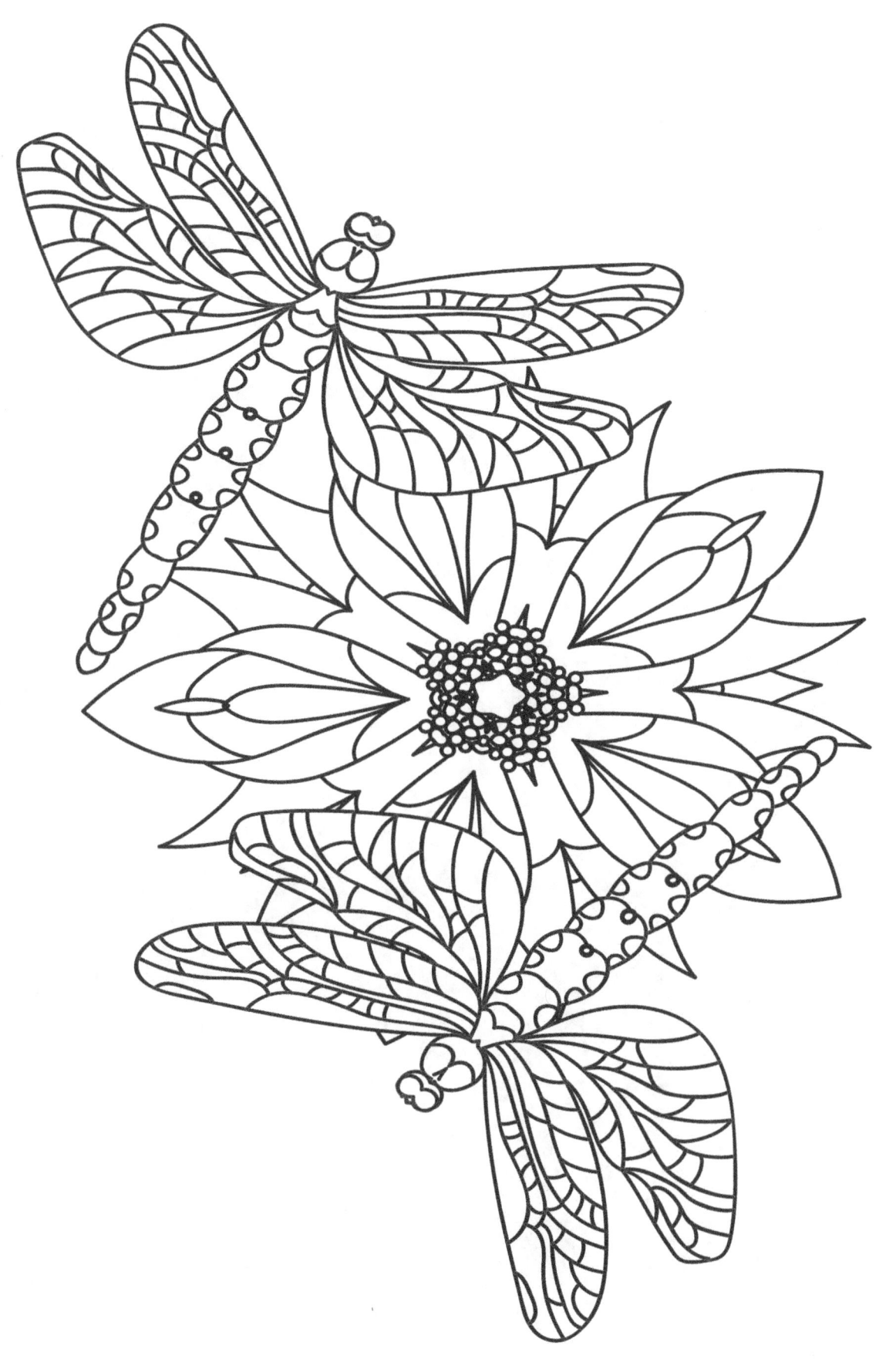

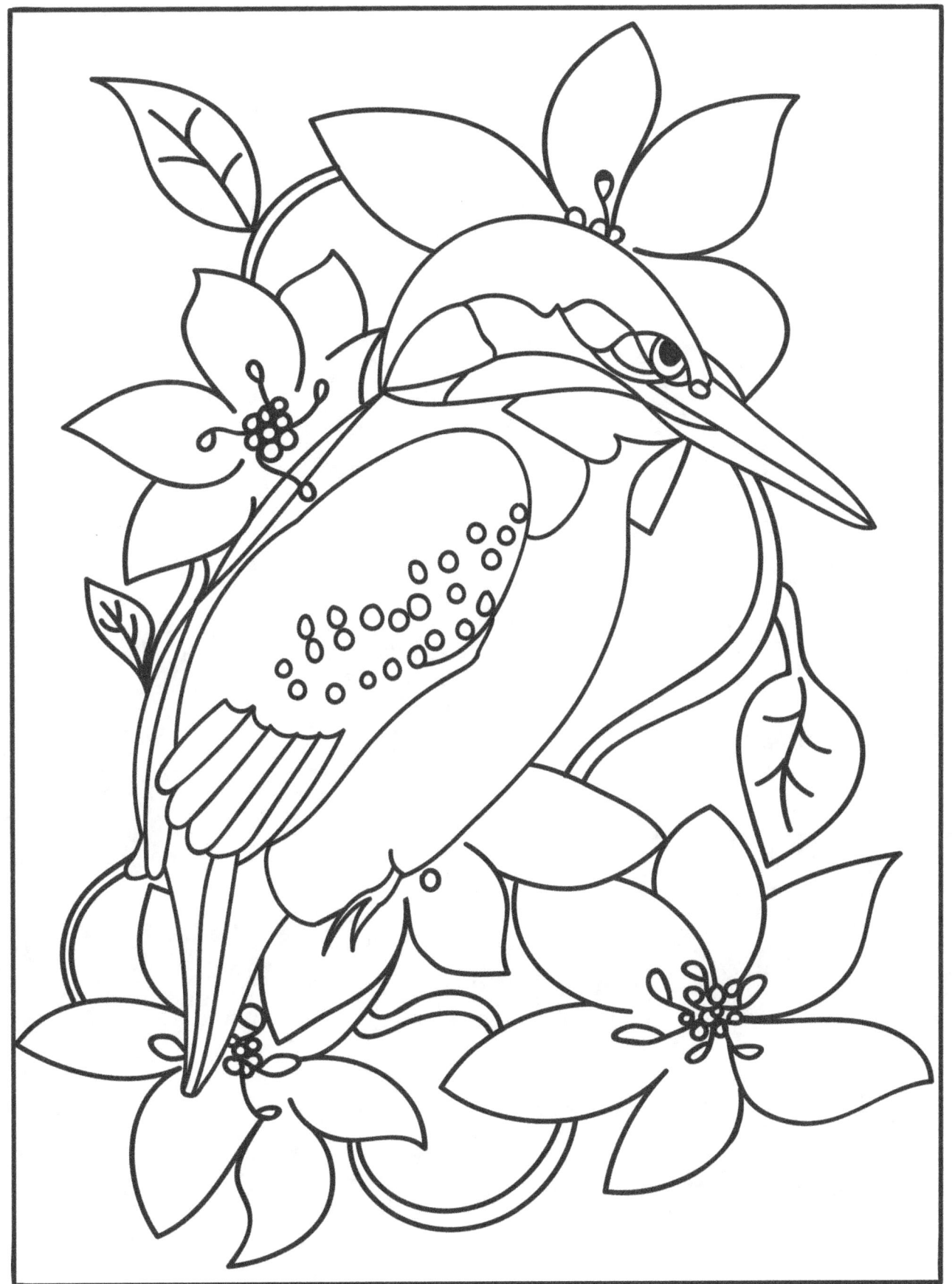

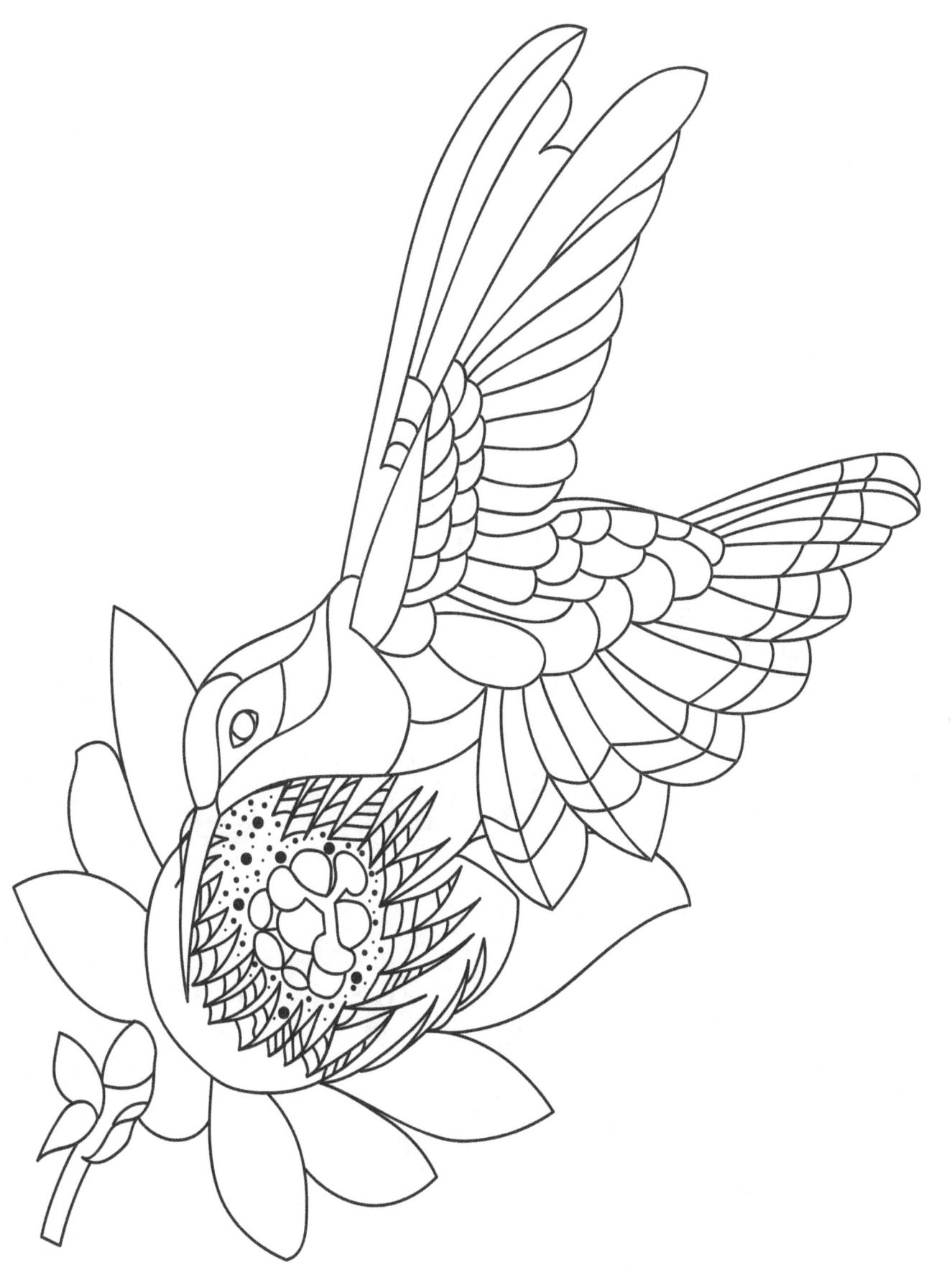

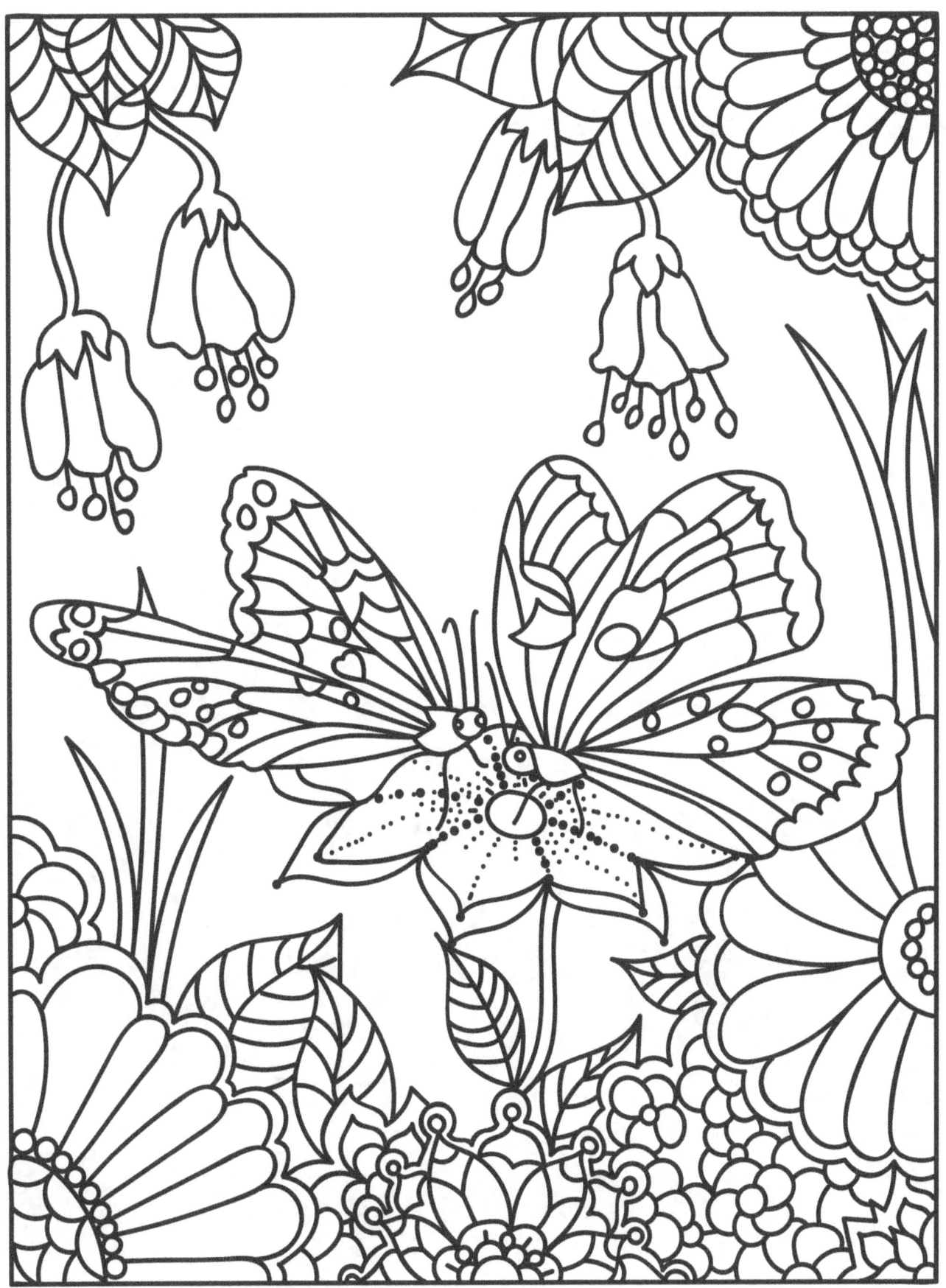

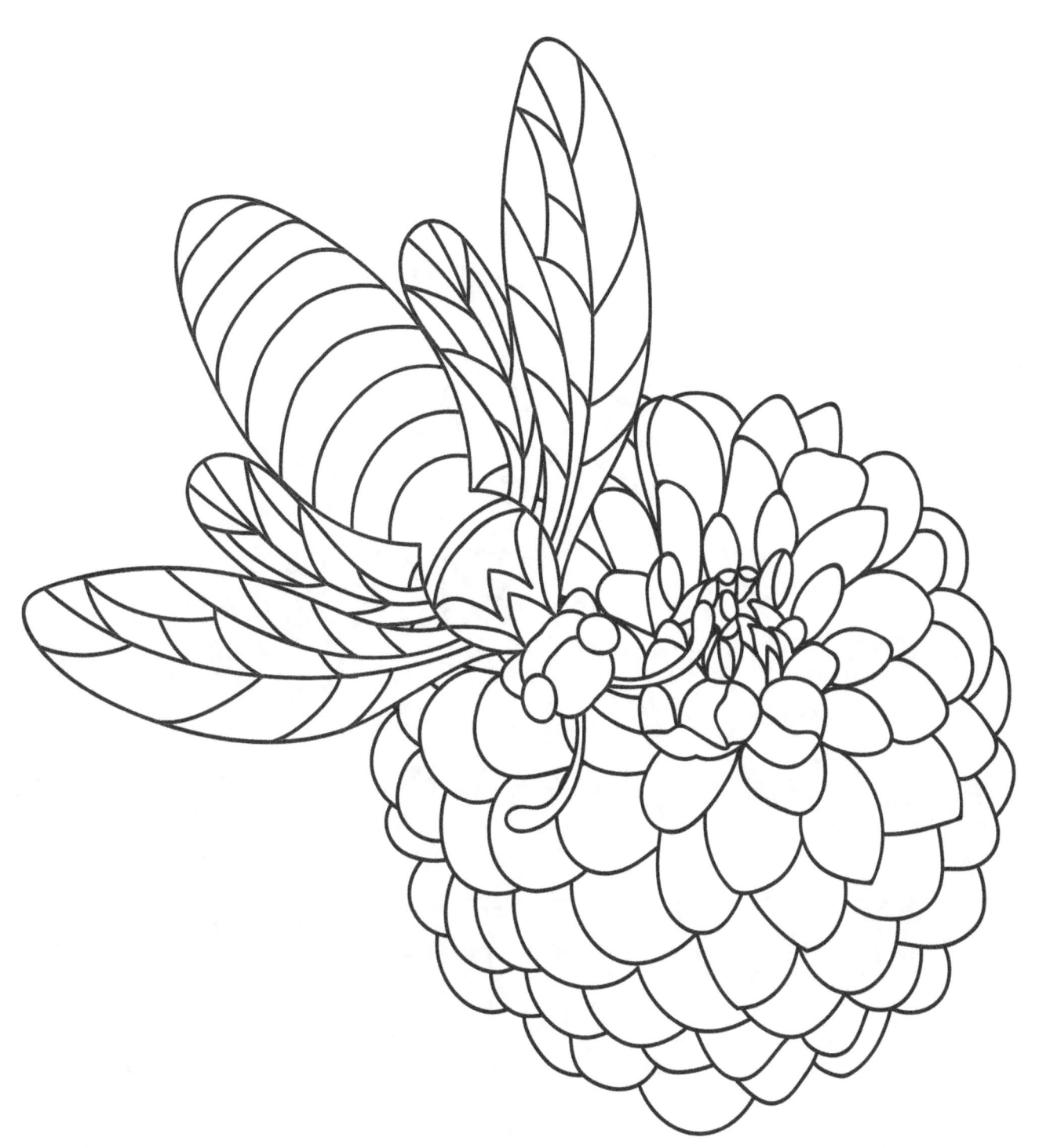

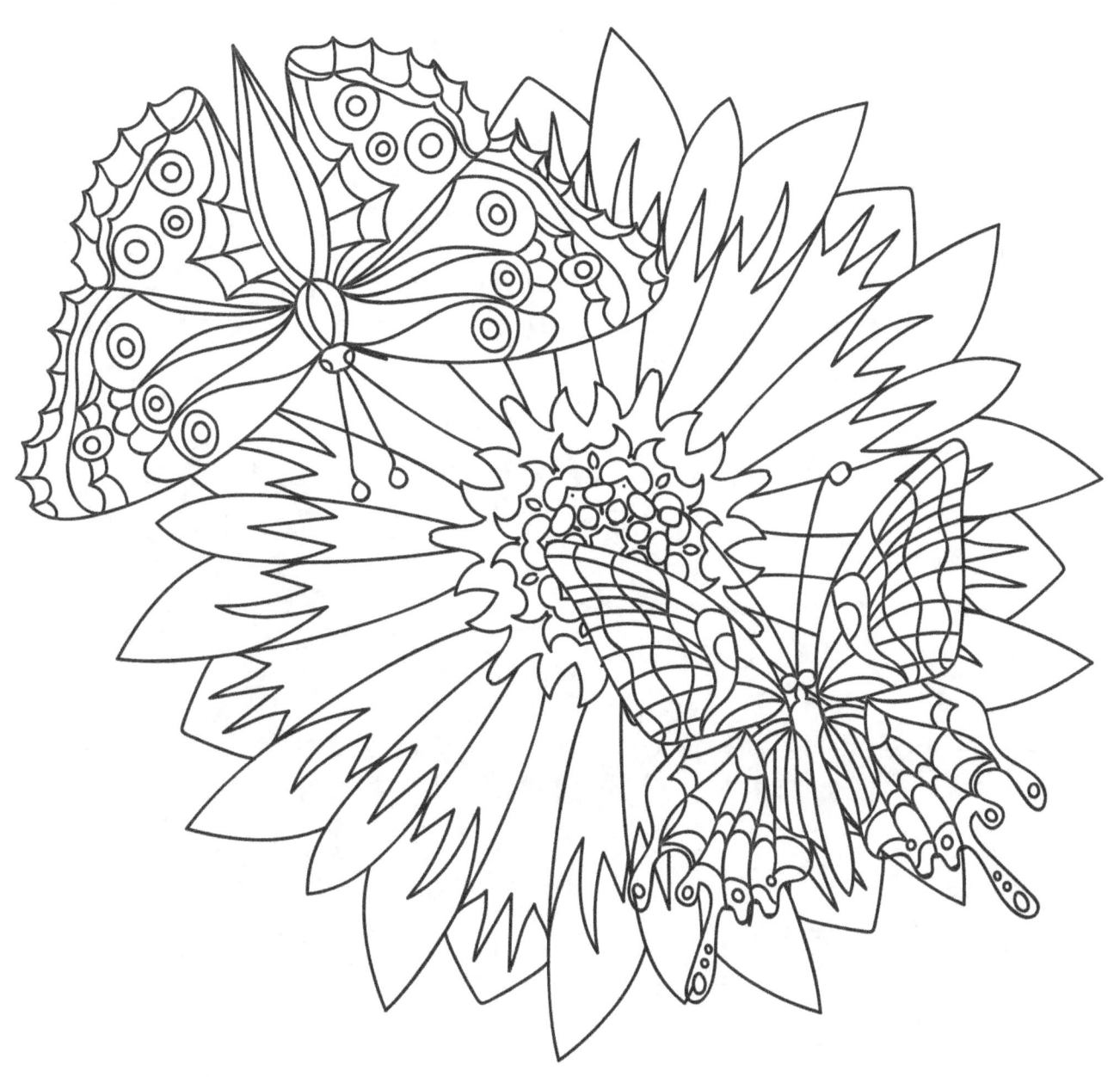

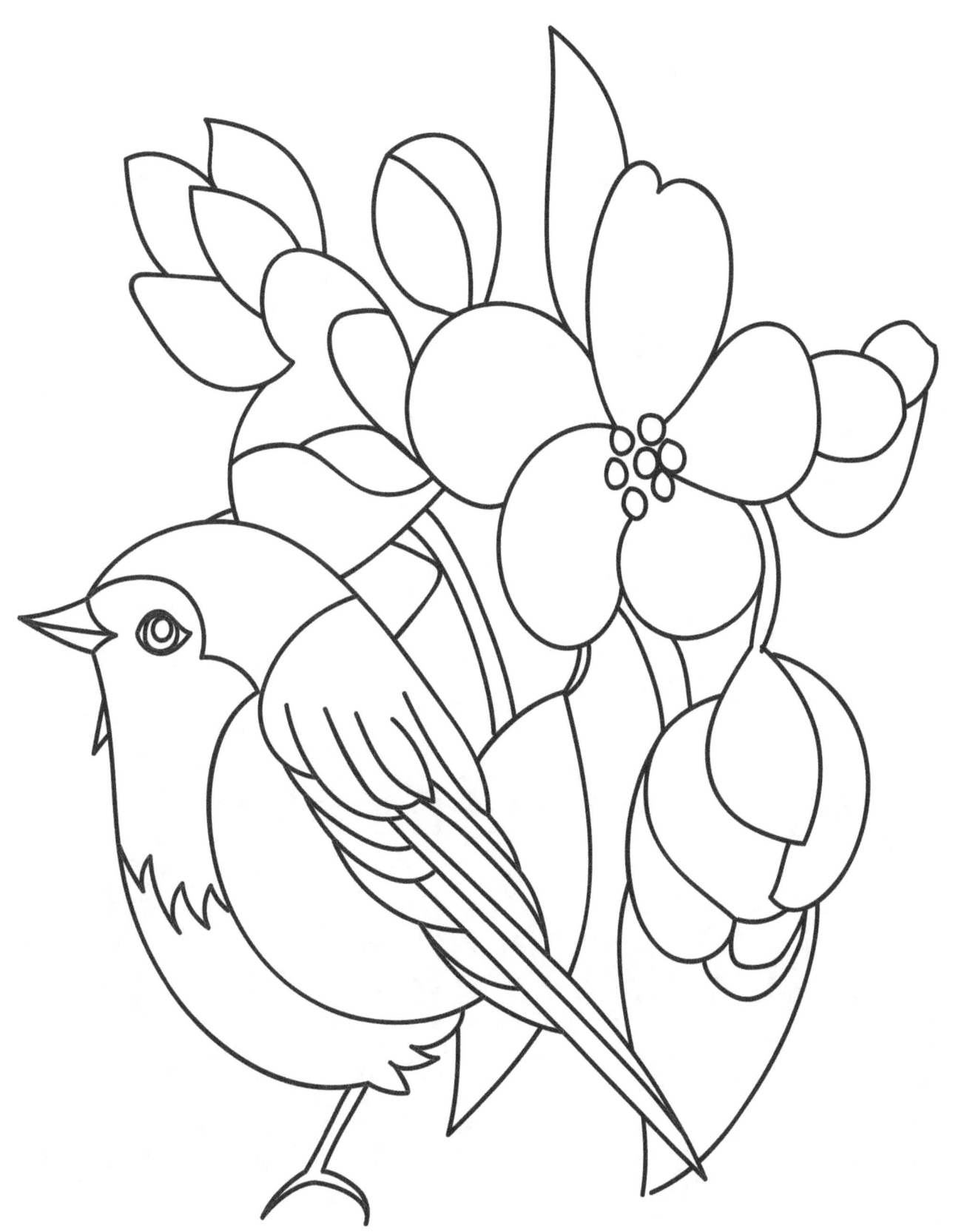

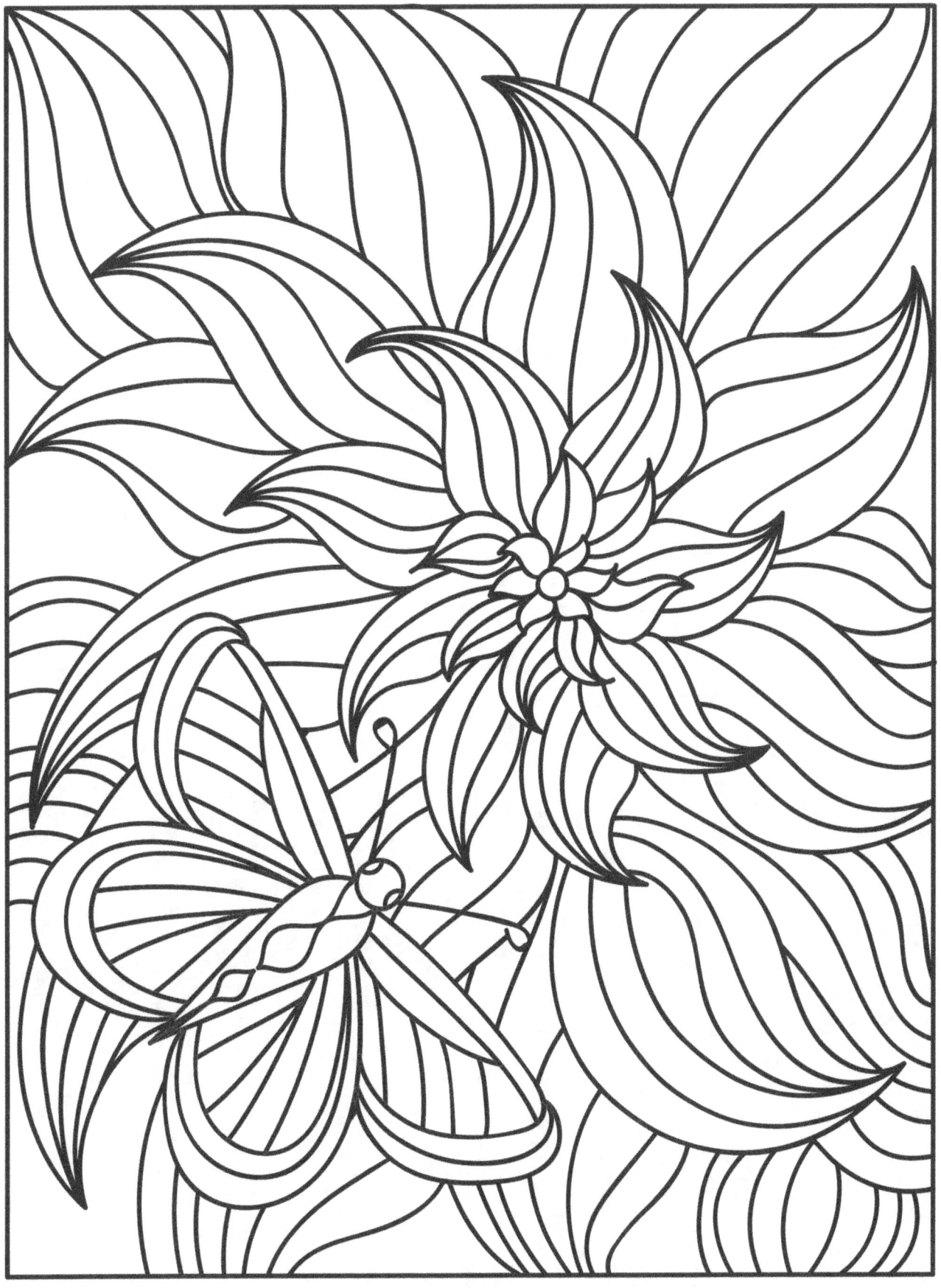

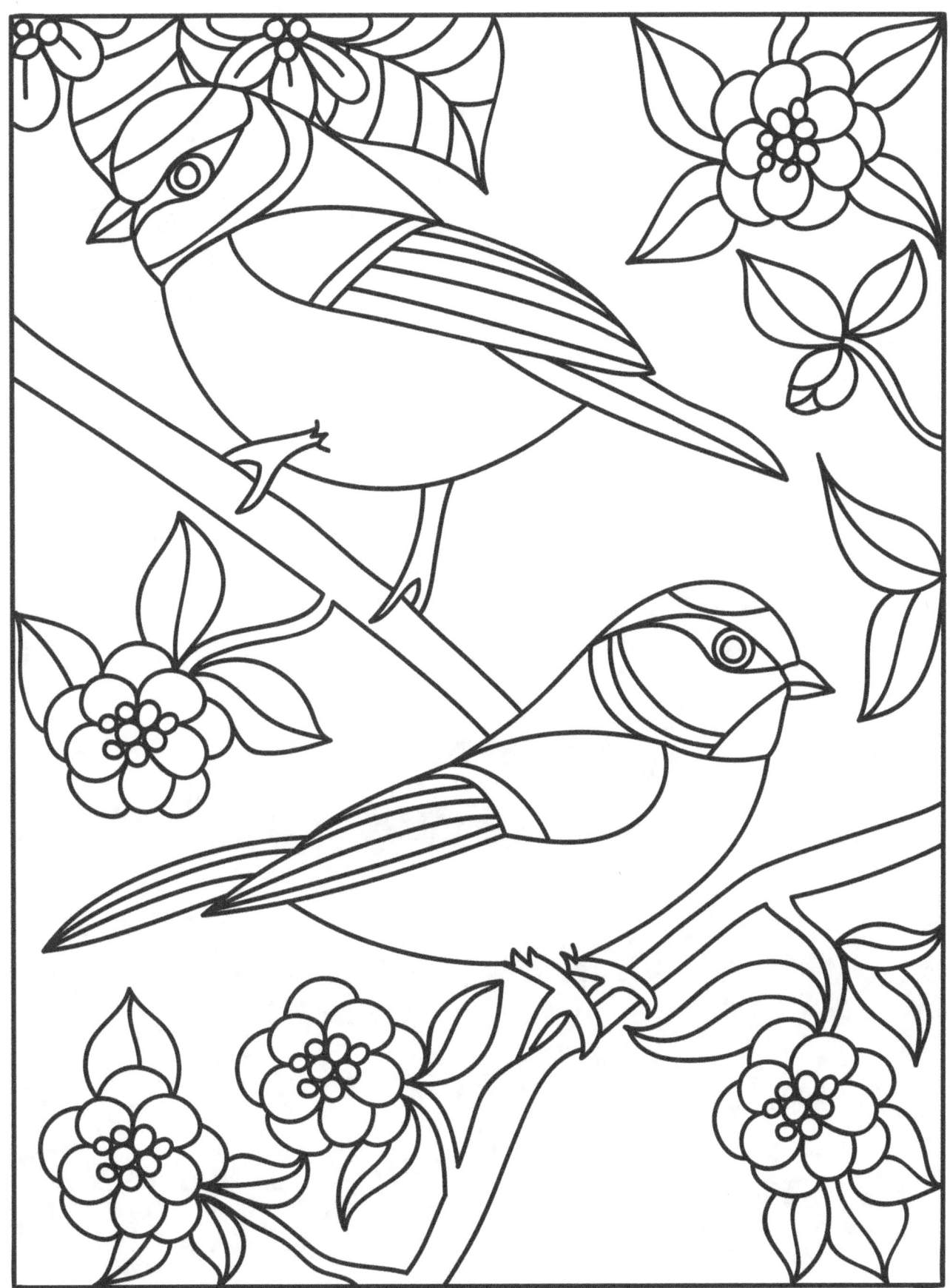

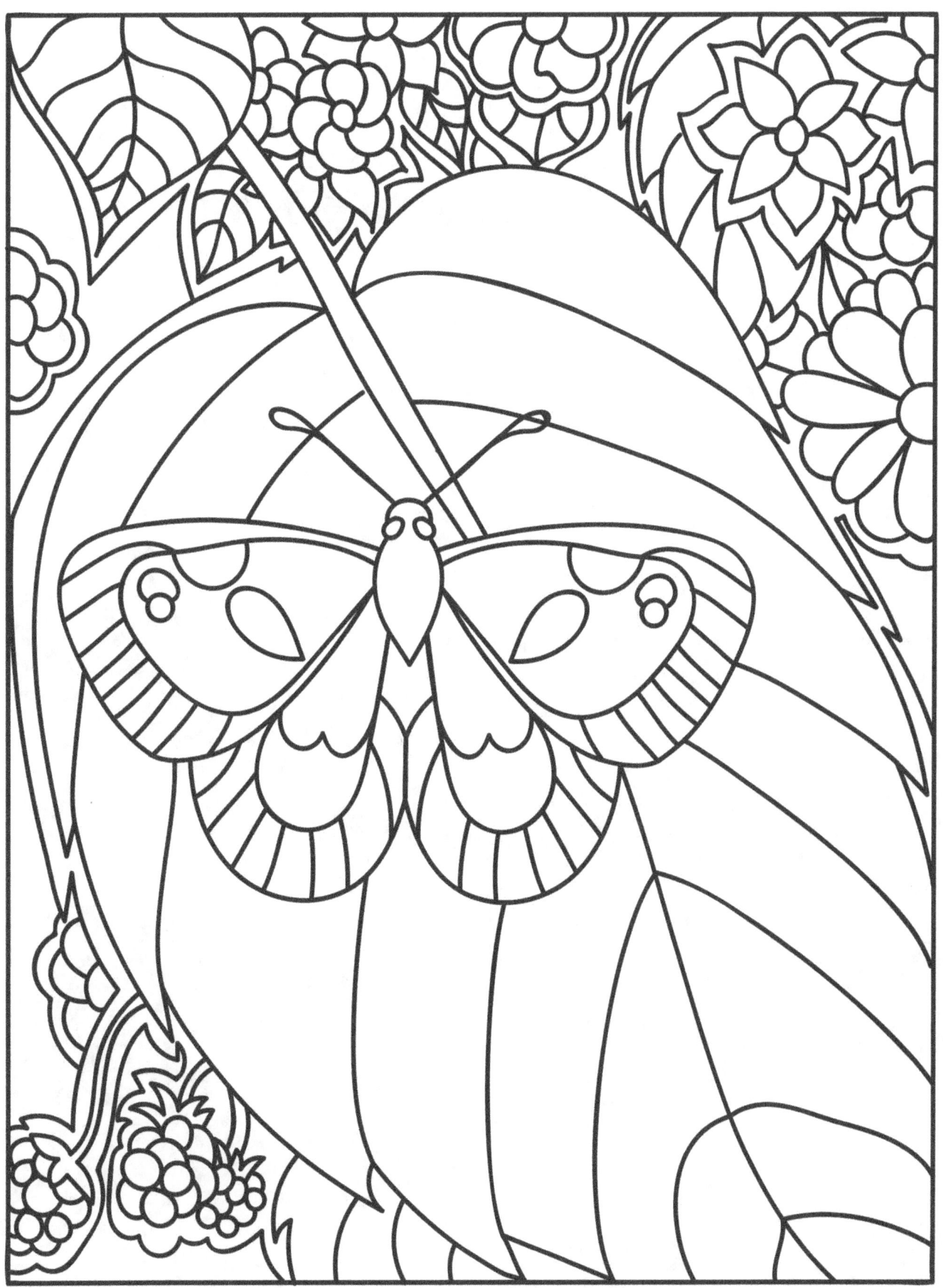

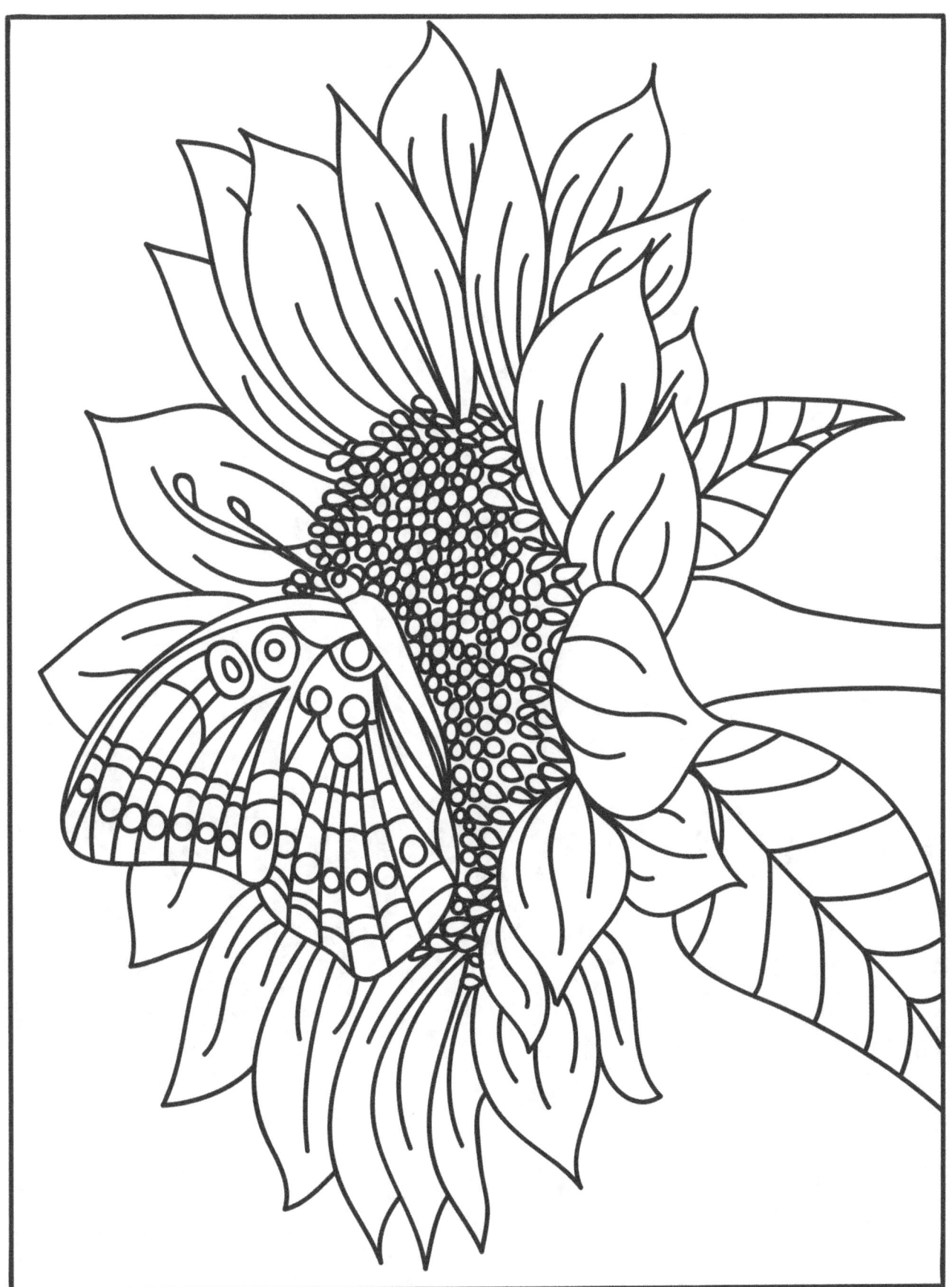

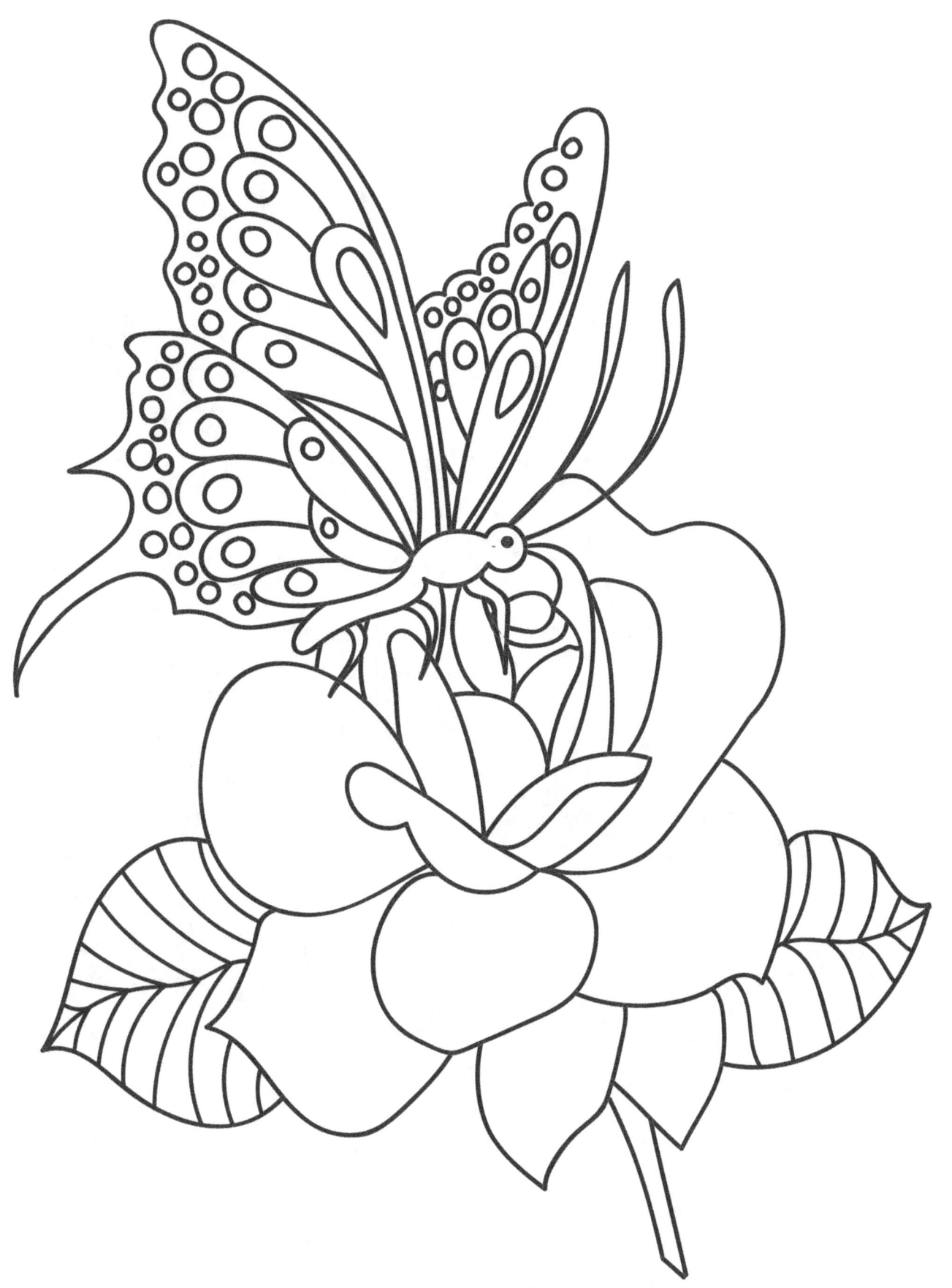

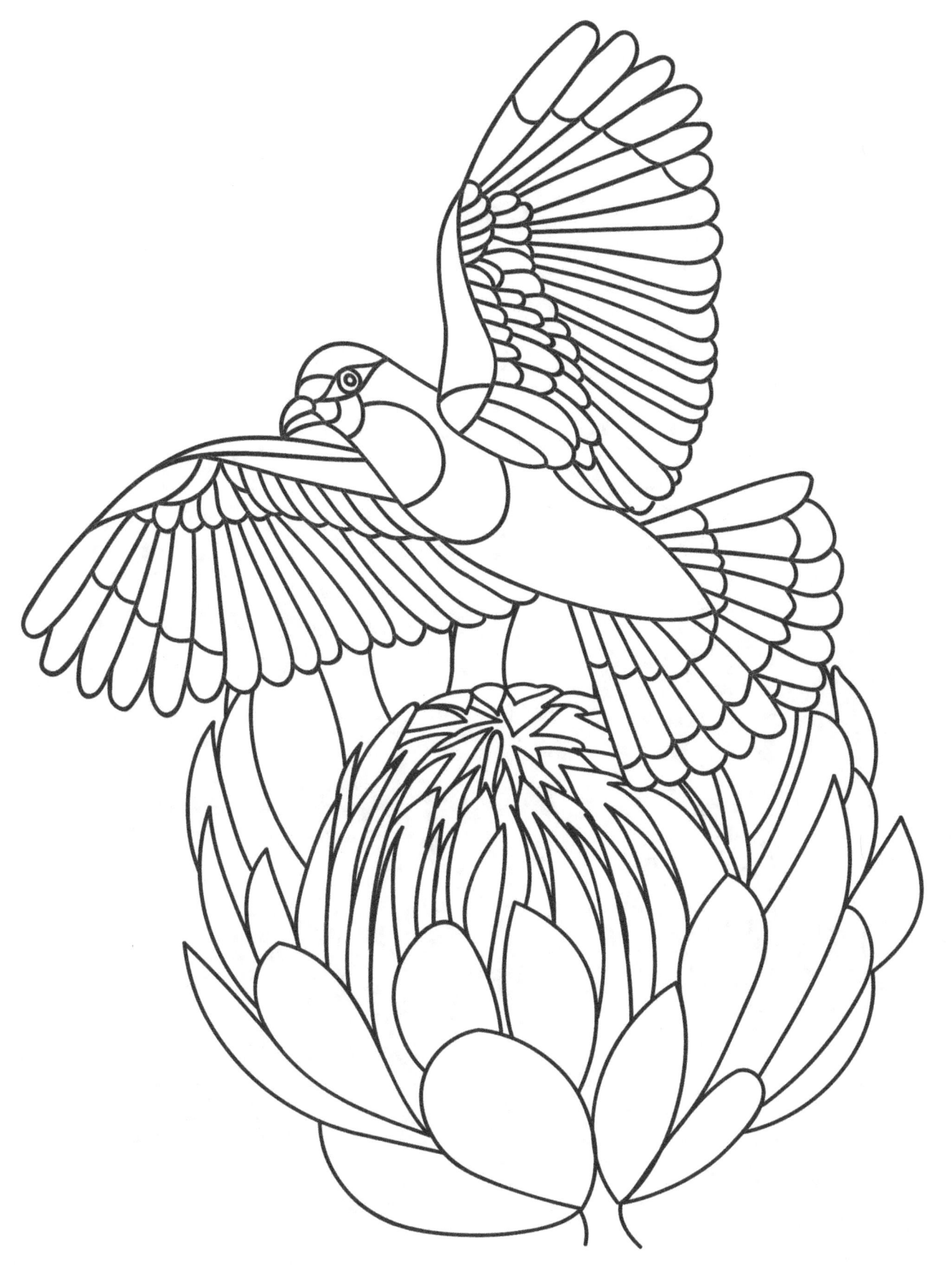

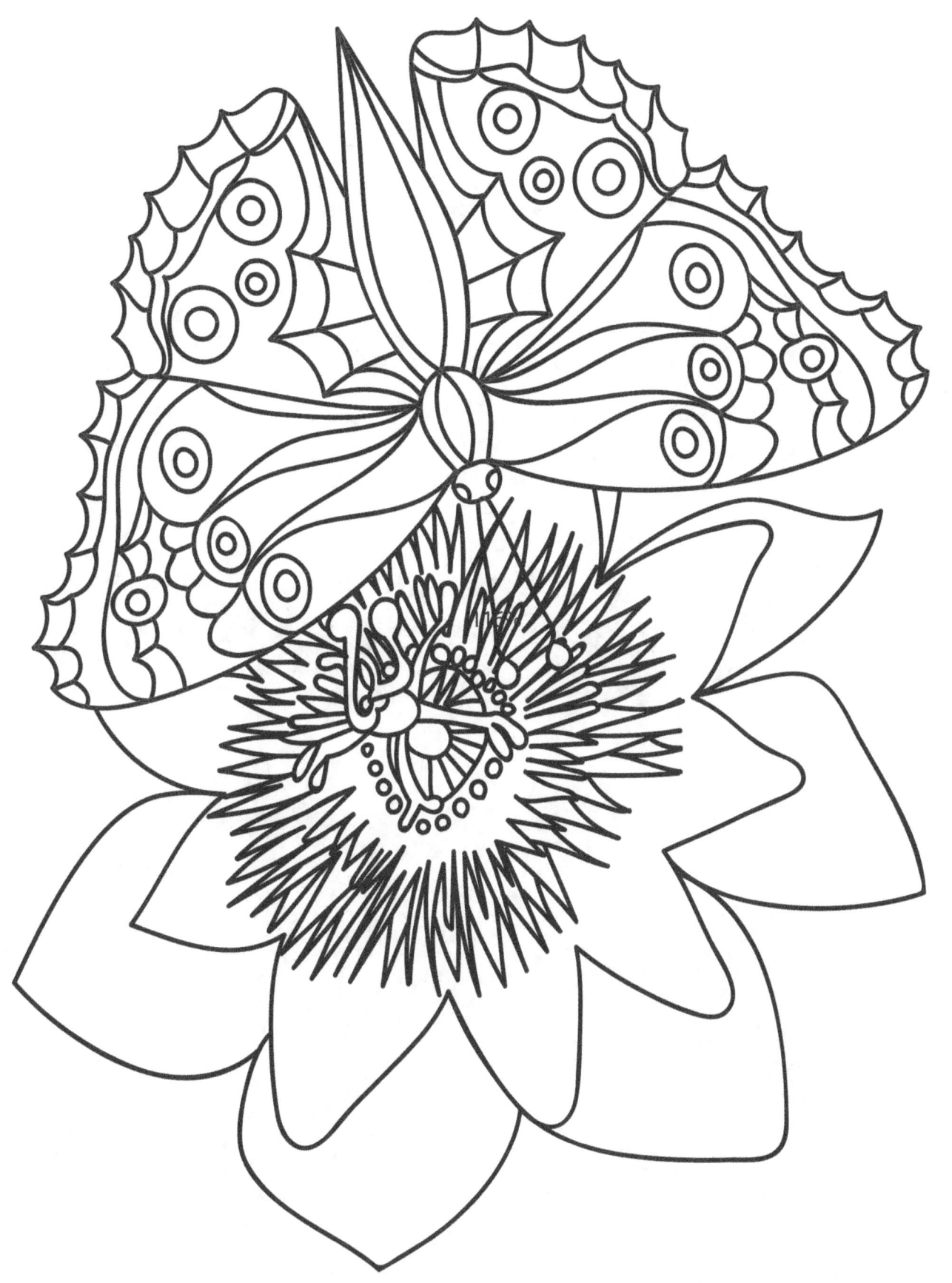

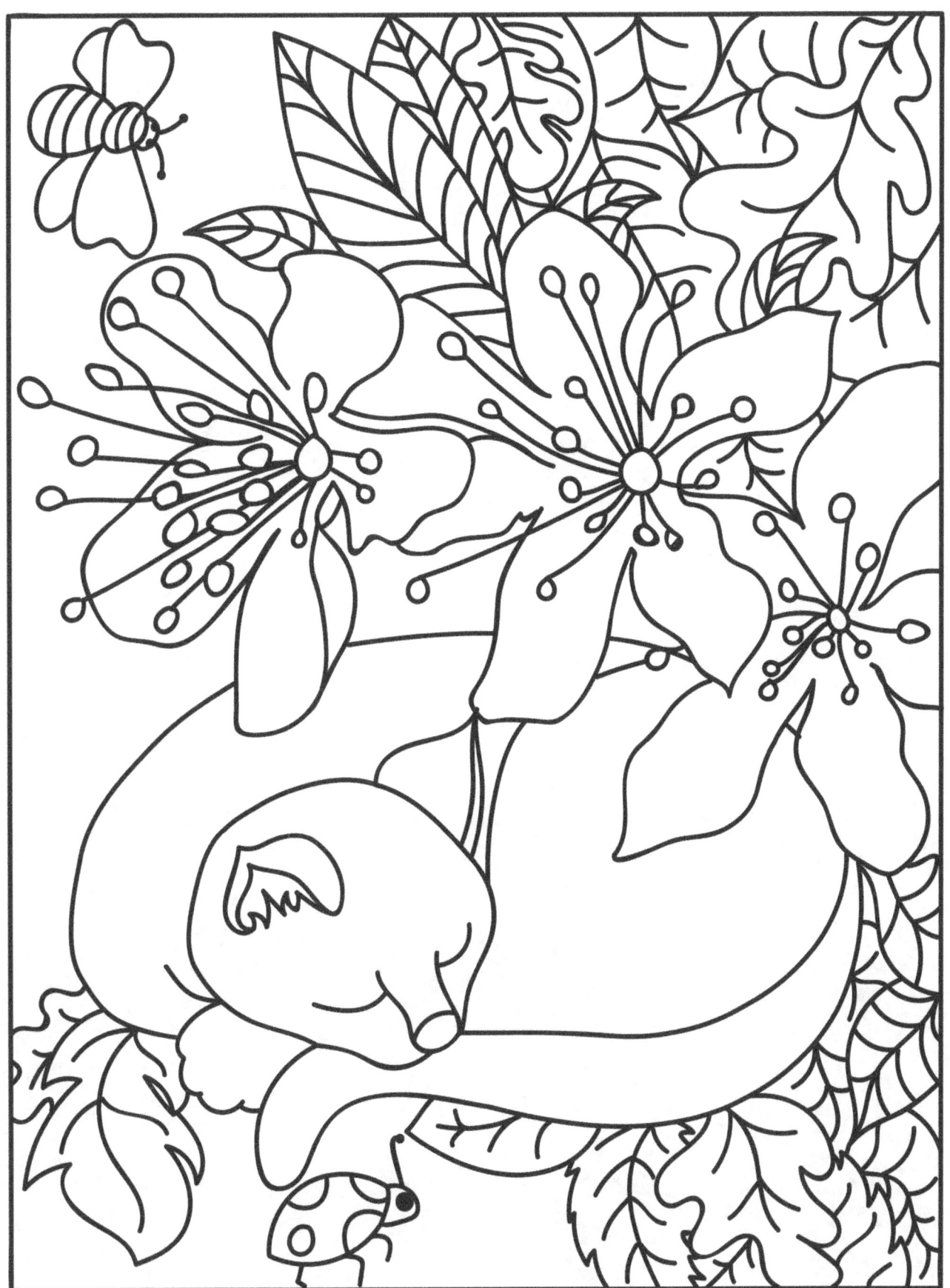

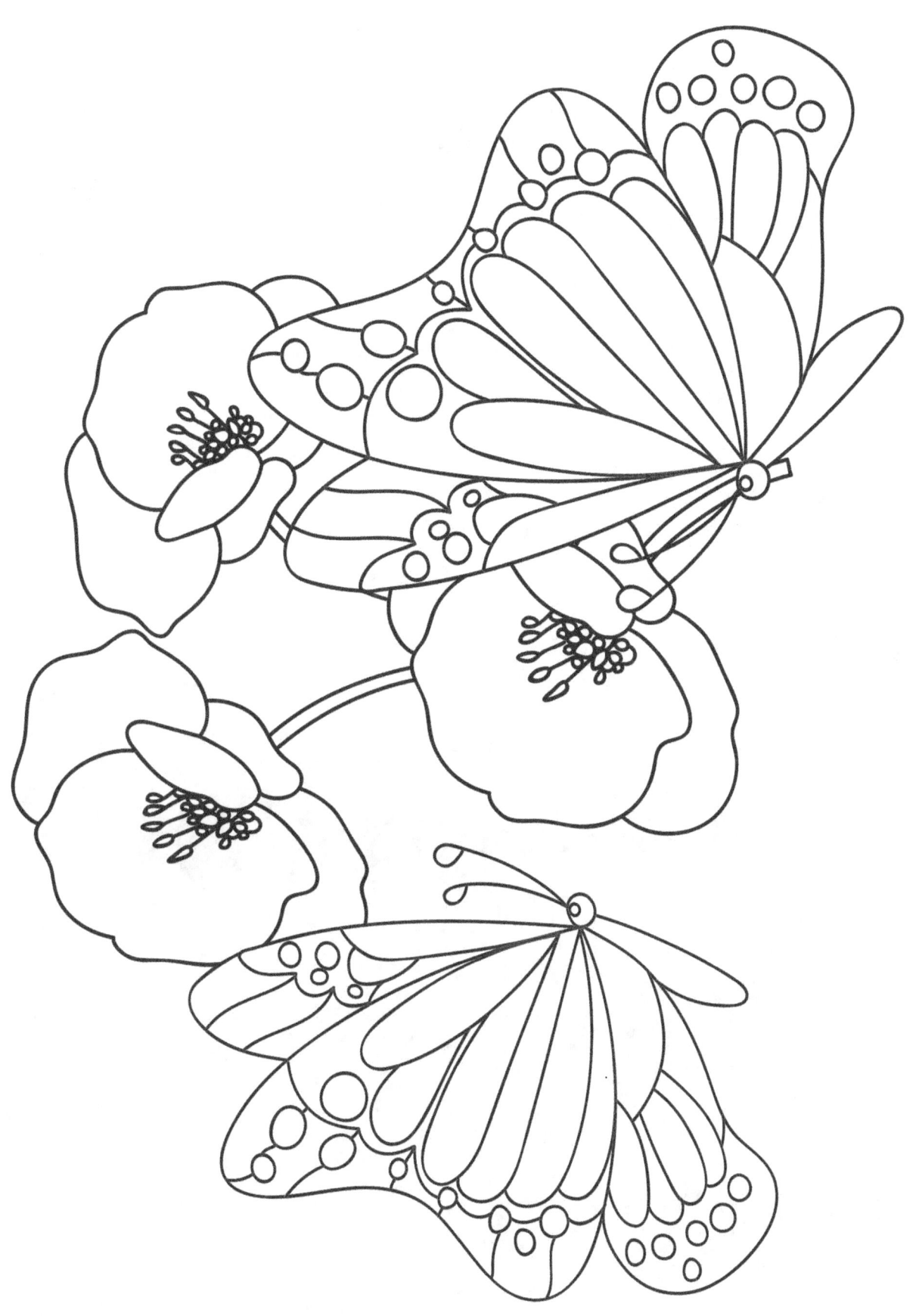

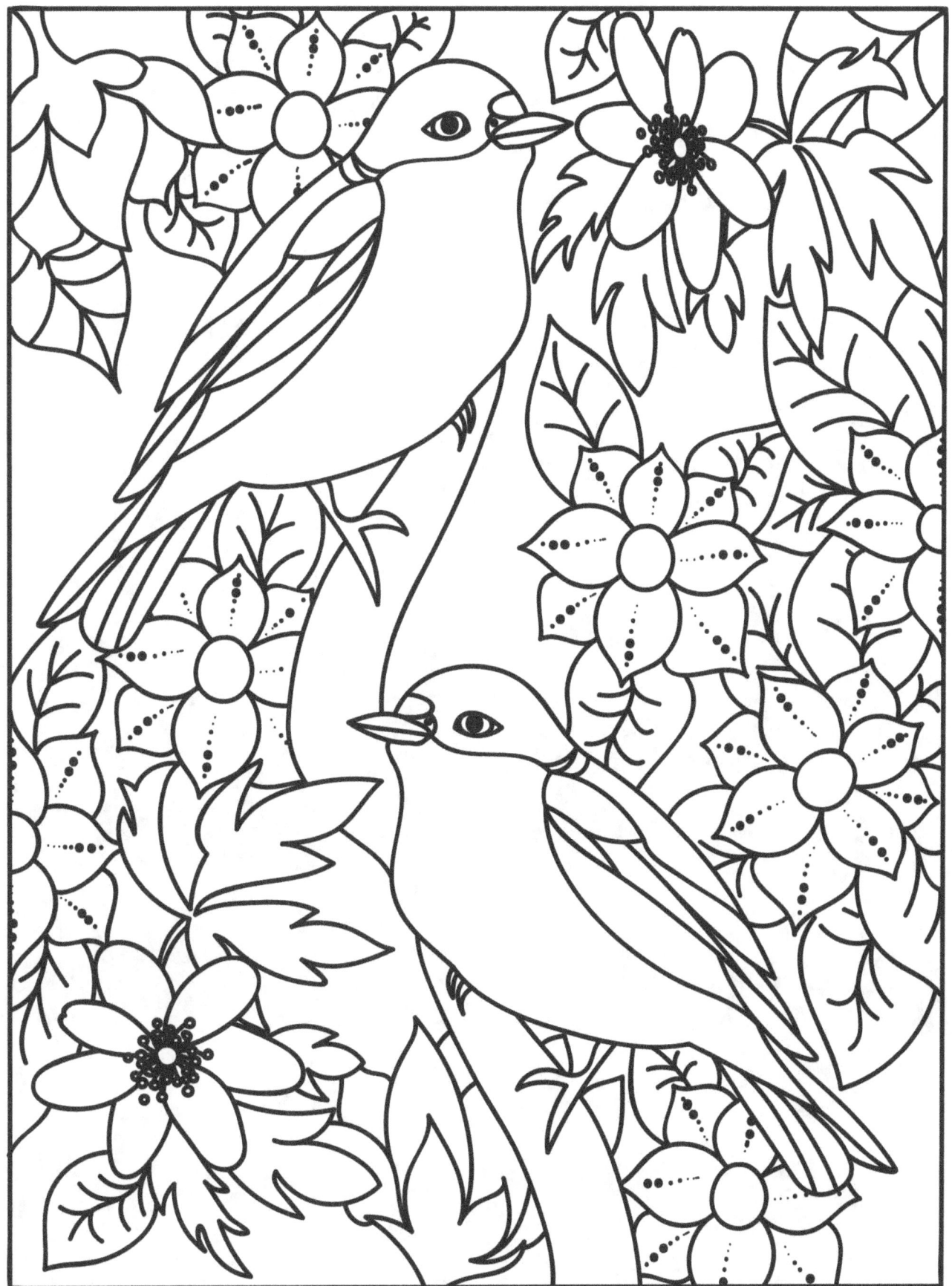

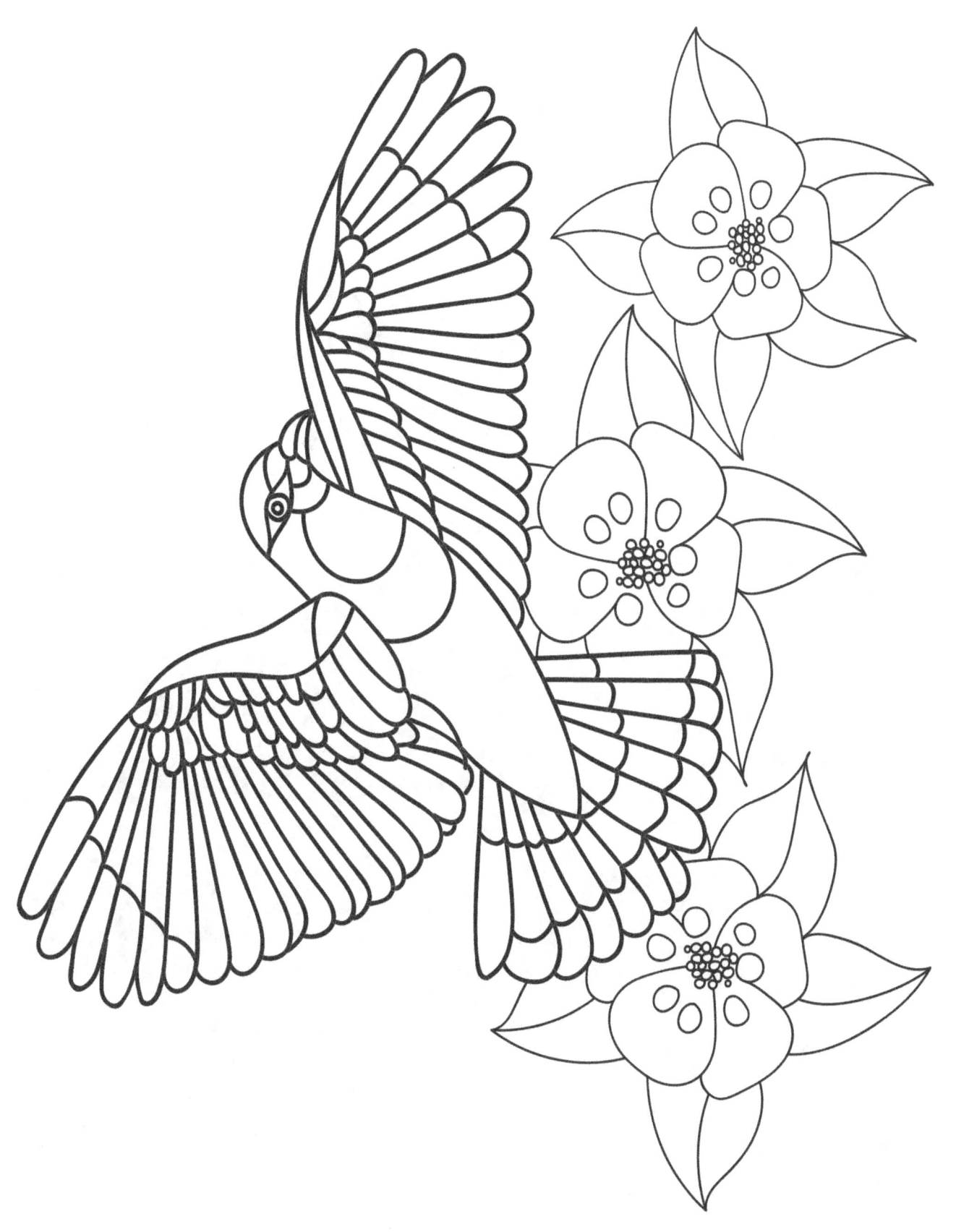

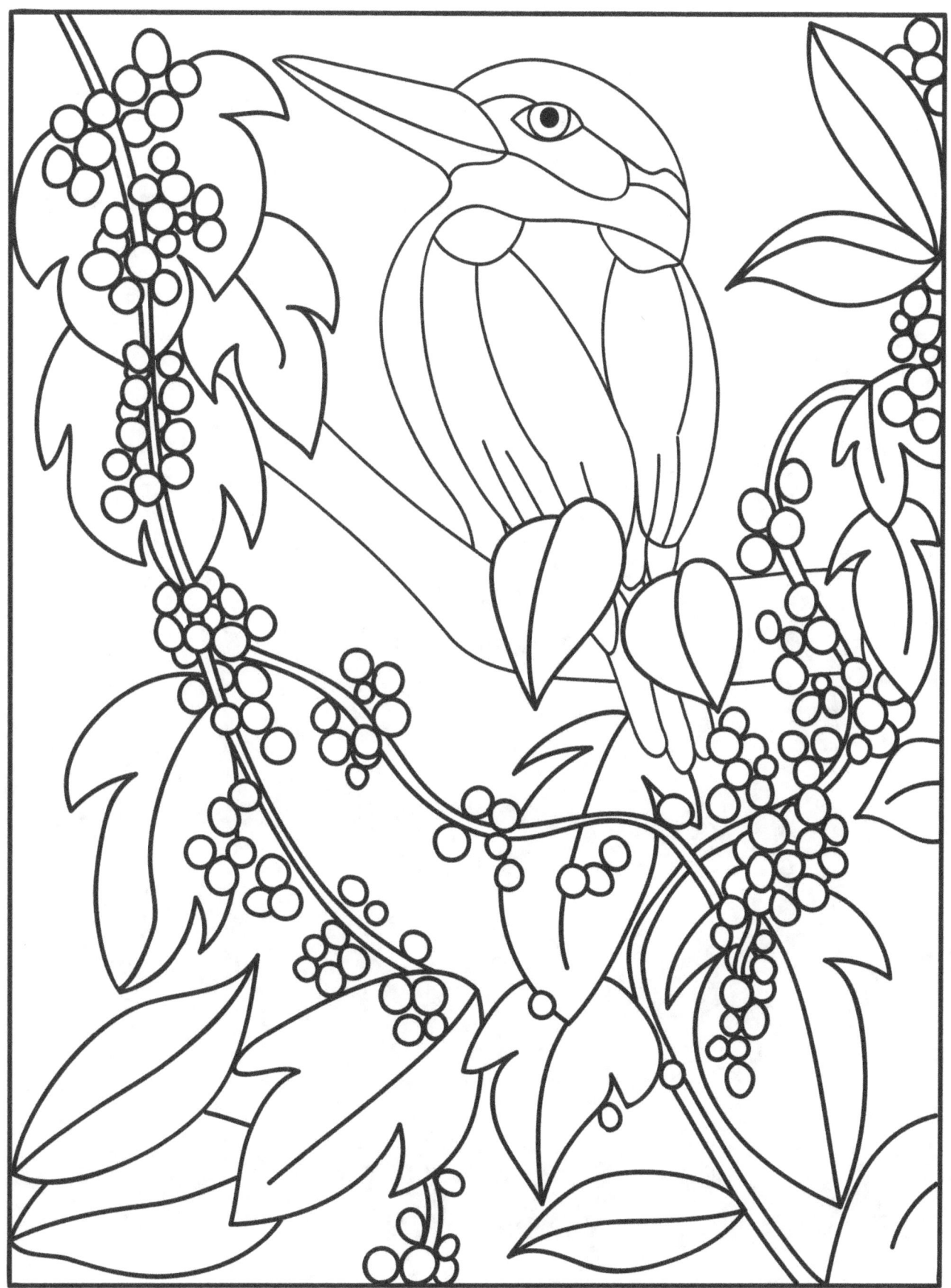

COLOR TEST PAGE

COLOR TEST PAGE

www.ingramcontent.com/pod-product-compliance
Lightning Source LLC
Chambersburg PA
CBHW081015170526
45158CB00010B/3054